MW00762721

CROSS✦ROADS

MORALITY

Teaching Guide

BROWN-ROA
A Division of Harcourt Brace & Company

BROWN-ROA
A Division of Harcourt Brace & Company

O u r   M i s s i o n

The primary mission of BROWN-ROA is to provide the
Catholic and Christian educational markets with the
highest quality catechetical print and media resources.
The content of these resources reflects the best insights
of current theology, methodology, and pedagogical research.
The resources are practical and easy to use, designed to meet
expressed market needs, and written to reflect the
teachings of the Catholic Church.

Nihil Obstat
Rev. Richard L. Schaefer

Imprimatur
✠ Most Rev. Jerome Hanus, O.S.B.
Archbishop of Dubuque
January 4, 1998
Feast of Saint Elizabeth Ann Seton

The Imprimatur is an official declaration that a book or pamphlet is free of doctrinal or moral error.
No implication is contained therein that anyone who granted the Imprimatur agrees with the
contents, opinions, or statements expressed.

Copyright © 1999 by BROWN-ROA, a division of Harcourt Brace & Company

All rights reserved. No part of this publication may be reproduced or transmitted in any form or by any
means, electronic or mechanical, including photocopy, recording, or any information storage and
retrieval system, without permission in writing from the publisher.

Permission is hereby granted to reproduce Chapter Quizzes and Final Test in this publication in complete
pages for instructional use and not for resale by any teacher using *Crossroads Morality*.

Portions of this work were published in previous editions.

The *Crossroads* program was written by Richard Reichert. The lesson plans were developed by Janie
Gustafson, Ph.D.

Illustrations (Student edition pages)
Rob Suggs

Photo Credits (Student edition pages)
Nancy Anne Dawe—57; Robert Fried—16, 32, 41, 45; Robert Cushman Hayes—24, 35, 51;
Mary Messenger—14; James L. Shaffer—2, 7, 8, 37, 42, 61, 67, 79, 81, 85, 86, 90; Robert Roethig— 22, 30;
Skjold Photography—68; D. Jeanene Tiner—20, 50, 52; Jim Whitmer—10, 12, 63

Printed in the United States of America

ISBN 0-15-950475-9

10   9   8   7   6

CROSS✦ROADS

MORALITY

Introductory Materials

Lesson Procedures

Concluding Materials

About the program...

Introduction

The *Crossroads* program is built upon three principal goals:

1. To provide a series of courses that takes into account the interests, needs, limits, and capacities of adolescents.
2. To provide a program designed specifically for the varied religious education structures, allowing for great flexibility without sacrificing scope or depth of content.
3. To provide a realistic approach that will ensure effective parental involvement in the religious education of youth.

Readable texts

To interest early adolescents in religion, the student text must use their language and present material on the level at which they are capable of relating.

Too often middle school and junior high religion texts are written for the teacher. A textbook is a teaching tool. Its effectiveness lies solely in the student's willingness to read it. Therefore the text must be enjoyable, interesting, and conversational. It must avoid religious jargon as much as possible. At the same time it must not pander religion by being too slangy or "hip." For these reasons, the student texts in this program avoid religious clichés and the stiff rhetoric of academic textbooks. Instead they are conversational and personal.

Short-range goals and measurable results

Younger adolescents are pragmatists. They want to see results. They are also impatient. They want to see results soon. They like change and become easily bored if things drag on. We've designed this program in light of these needs. Each course is short, taking only eight weeks to cover a topic. Each course is self-contained. At the end of the course, students will be able to see the results of their work.

Then it's on to a new topic and a new challenge. You don't have to sustain student interest in one text or one topic through an entire year. Nevertheless each course does provide a comprehensive treatment of its particular topic. The courses present "meat and potatoes," not fluff or busywork. Individual courses blend with each other and support each other, but each course can stand alone. Hence there is a sense of newness as each course is introduced. There is an end in sight, just eight short weeks away. For anyone who has worked with adolescents, the appeal of this format is self-evident.

Flexibility

These short-term, self-contained courses can be adapted to just about any existing school or parish religious education structure. They also open many new programming possibilities for the creative program director.

Each class has certain learning goals. Something measurable is accomplished at each class session. Students are held accountable. This technique increases motivation to use time well. And because students feel they are accomplishing something, they don't approach classes as a waste of time (a common complaint among many younger adolescent religious education students).

In a different vein, the short-term nature of the courses allows you to make optimum use of the limited number of times you can meet each year. Eight weeks usually provides ample time to cover a given topic in sufficient depth for this age group. (If it were much shorter, you'd run the risk of only skimming the surface. Staying much longer on one topic prevents you from introducing other equally essential topics for this stage of faith development. It also runs the risk of beginning to bore the students.)

Parent Involvement

Everyone agrees that we need parent involvement to make our religion classes truly effective. The approach of this program takes this into account in its

- Seeing to it that—when that hour comes around each week—the youth does, in fact, sit down and do the homework.
- Taking about ten minutes after the homework is completed to

Ironically if parents can attain just that minimum of involvement in their youth's religious education, they are maximizing the effectiveness of the class and the teacher's efforts. That same simple involvement sends a clear message to the youth that the parent considers religious education an important value—every bit on a par with math and other subjects the youth is studying.

A textbook is a teaching tool. It's effectiveness relies solely in the student's willingness to read it.

expectation that youth do about one hour of homework for every hour spent in class. This is a critical feature to the success of the program. This supervision may take several forms:

- Determining with the youth which hour each week is going to be set aside for reviewing the chapter and doing homework.
- Effective parental involvement simply means that the parent(s)/guardian(s) exercise routine supervision in the matter of homework.

check on how well the youth actually completed the assignment.

In other words, parental involvement simply requires two things: *helping the youth set up a routine for doing homework* and then *taking a few minutes to check on how well the homework was done.* Demanding that homework be done is a routine parental task. Even the busiest parent can usually find ten minutes each week to check on how well the homework was done.

Summary

The *Crossroads* program seeks to achieve a balance between a clearly academic religious education program and an informal, practical, experiential one. The program is academic in that students are expected to master specific material; they are held accountable for this mastery, just as in any other academic subject. The program is informal in that the text itself is conversational rather than pedantic. The suggested lesson plans encourage student involvement and require minimal lecturing on the part of the teacher.

Hopefully your own approach in teaching the course will maintain that same balance. Make clear to your students that you have expectations of them and that they have "work" to do. But strive to temper this business-like approach with warmth, spontaneity, and personal interest. To the degree that you can achieve this balance, your course will come close to achieving the ultimate in religious education—making learning both meaningful and fun!

Early Adolescents:
A partial profile and implications for catechesis

Many books that analyze and describe adolescents have been written. Yet these students are often misunderstood. Teachers tend to stereotype them as a "tough group to teach," especially when it comes to religion.

The following ideas focus on selected parts of the information that have been gathered about this age group. We have tried to identify those factors that are most helpful in understanding how to relate to early adolescents and how to present the Catholic faith to them.

Psychospiritual development

In terms of religious education, the single most important thing to realize about early adolescent youth (eleven-to-fifteen-year-olds) is that they still experience the world as two-dimensional. They are very much at home with the physical or the tangible (the first dimension of reality). Also their capacity for abstract thinking at the level of logic and deductive reasoning (the second dimension of reality) is developing almost to the adult level. But the world of the spiritual or

metaphysical (the third dimension of reality) still eludes them. Early adolescents lack the capacity for full spiritual insight, a capacity that will not emerge for several more years. In that sense, the typical fourteen-year-old has more in common with nine-year-olds than with sixteen-year-olds. In terms of psychospiritual development, early adolescents are still children.

The most common mistake (and the reason so many good catechists experience frustration in working with this age group) is to expect too much of eleven-to-fifteen-year-olds. It is an understandable mistake. They can seem like "little adults." Many have already gone through puberty and its growth spurt. In terms of their logic and their capacity to organize, they have virtually the same capacity as adults. They are so good at logical thinking, in fact, that it is just about impossible to out-argue them! However, adult faith is not logical, and it cannot be totally defended at the level of logic. In terms of faith, early adolescents are not yet adults. They have not yet obtained full-blown faith (spiritual insight into mystery).

Adult faith is rooted in the experience of mystery. For example, consider the Beatitudes or the mystery of the cross or concepts such as evil, sin, and mercy. It is possible to talk about these realities in a logical way, but ultimately our human words fail. These truths lie beyond human definitions. We can experience them at the level

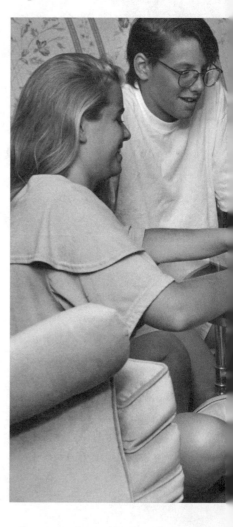

of spiritual insight. To talk about these mysteries effectively within the faith community, we appeal to the symbolic, the sacramental, the analogical.

Adult faith consists of a "vision" of reality that can never be fully articulated. It is precisely this experience of mystery that excites and motivates us. We seek to proclaim and share this faith vision in our catechesis.

Thus we may view catechesis at the middle school and junior high level as still foundational.

We need to let them know there is another whole dimension to reality.

It prepares youth for adult faith, adult motivation, and adult response to the gospel, but it does not seek to effect adult faith and motivation. At this age level, we can and should present the vision and the ideal within our catechesis. We can and should also witness to our own excitement and commitment to the gospel as we catechize. But we should not expect the youth to respond in kind, to understand fully, or to appreciate what it is we share. Authentic spiritual insight (adult faith) is still several years beyond them.

Initially, many teachers tend to balk at this because they think it would mean "watering down" the richness of faith. Such teachers fully expect early adolescents to respond with the same level of insight and enthusiasm as they themselves bring to the subject. But the early adolescents do not respond, and they cannot. Consequently they respond quite predictably: They show boredom; they do not enter into discussion or class activities; they are mischievous; they complain about how "dumb" the classes are; they become picky, arguing about everything the teacher presents.

In reality, eleven-to-fifteen-year-olds can be a delightful group with which to work, provided we enter into their two-dimensional world and present our topics in a two-dimensional way. Granted, there is room for holding up the vision and for calling early adolescents to the ideal. (We need to let them know there is another whole dimension to reality. They will even be able, on occasion, to catch small glimpses of that reality.) But the major portion of our effort should be focused on the tangible and logical aspects of our faith.

The fact that early adolescents are still children in terms of their psychospiritual development is the key, then, for determining both what we should present and what methods will be most effective. Methods that involve logic (problem solving, organizing, deducting a conclusion, applying principles of cause and effect) will usually be more popular than those requiring symbolism and imagery. That's why most students this age are more apt to enjoy academic subjects such as math and science than subjects such as literature and poetry. Appreciation for the latter depends largely upon a capacity for spiritual insight.

This age group also prefers hands-on activities and projects that produce tangible results over those that involve abstract discussion, reflection, and long-range results. They tend to be pragmatists and doers, not philosophers. They seek practical information more than abstract ideals.

Other significant characteristics of early adolescents

Understanding early adolescents as two-dimensional is the key to effective catechesis for this age group. However there are several other significant characteristics of development that we should keep in mind if we are to relate effectively to students this age.

Identity. Eleven-to-fifteen-year-olds feel a strong inner drive to reject certain aspects of their earlier childhood. At the same time they are not fully committed to leaving behind some of the positive aspects of that earlier age (for example, a sense of security and a sense of freedom from responsibility).

This inner conflict accounts for a certain ambivalence early adolescents feel toward themselves, their parents, and other authority

figures. They no longer think of themselves as children, but they don't think of themselves as adults, either. They would like the safety and security of childhood, but they also want the freedom to explore and to make decisions for themselves. Consequently, they fluctuate frequently between childlike docility and a bullheaded defense of their rights to act for themselves.

One minute early adolescents are perfectly comfortable allowing their parents to make decisions for them. The next minute they protest that their parents are treating them "like babies." One minute these youth may display an emotional outburst of anger or tears appropriate for five-year-olds. The next minute they may display the logic and reasonableness of an adult. This inconsistency not only confuses parents and teachers, it confuses the youth as well. The resulting confusion gives rise to two other significant identity traits of this age group: insecurity and self-consciousness.

Social Development. In their effort to remove themselves from childhood, early adolescents tend to withdraw socially (and to some extent emotionally) from their parents. (Parents, after all, are the symbols of their childhood dependence and the source of their childhood identity.) Instead, eleven-to-fifteen-year-olds seek the companionship of peers. They unwittingly become dependent upon peers for approval and acceptance.

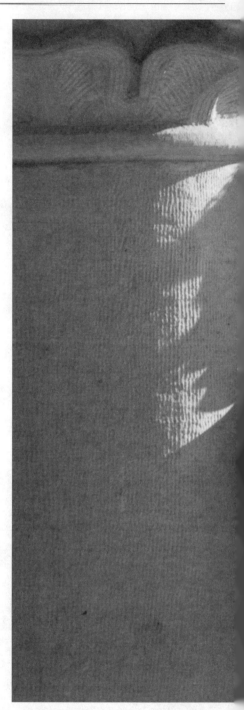

Because approval and acceptance are based more on externals than on inner worth, early adolescent students become very self-conscious about externals (physical size, clothes, hairstyles, and whatever fads are making the rounds). They become inhibited and lose much of the spontaneity that marked their earlier childhood. In the presence of their peer group, such as in a religion class,

experiences of this age group. As parents and teachers know, it's impossible to protect adolescents from some of this pain. Early adolescents are capable of an almost vicious cruelty toward one another, motivated more by their own insecurities than by any real viciousness. They constantly need to be challenged in this regard.

On the other hand, this same vulnerability to peer pressure and dependence upon group approval can be an advantage. If the teacher can guide the group to appreciate certain positive values and behaviors as "cool," the group will promote these values and behaviors among itself. (This approach has been used very effectively in some areas for combating the use of drugs and alcohol.)

In any event, personal insecurity, self-consciousness, and vulnerability to peer pressure are "facts of life" for this age group. We need to be sensitive to these realities as we plan our classes and conduct them. For example, activities that require too much self-disclosure or that potentially expose the individual student to ridicule are doomed to failure. Group activities—activities that solicit cooperation, involve wholesome competition, and allow for a certain degree of hiding within the anonymity of the group when responding—have a better chance of success.

Eleven-to-fifteen-year-olds feel a strong inner drive to reject certain aspects of their earlier childhood.

they are very cautious about what they say. They are more eager to say what the group thinks is "cool" than to say what they honestly feel. They can be easily pressured into behavior they know in their hearts is inappropriate.

Rejection and ridicule are two of the most painful and feared

Moral Development. The moral development of most early adolescents reflects their two-dimensional state of psycho-spiritual development. They approach morality at the level of the logical and the legalistic. Morality is a matter of strict justice. Good actions deserve rewards; bad actions deserve punishment. It's that simple. "That isn't fair" is the most common complaint of early adolescents. They have a terrible time with the parable of the laborers who came at different times of the day and yet all received the same reward.

A morality motivated by a spiritual vision of love, altruism, and mercy is still beyond most early adolescents. They may be able to understand such morality at the level of logic, but motivation to behave morally will remain, for the most part, rooted in legalism and in logical, causal relationships between certain bad actions and certain bad consequences. (An appeal against cheating in school that is based on the ideals of self-respect and personal integrity doesn't have much force if students observe that their peers are getting As by cheating while they are getting Cs as a result of their personal integrity.)

In the same way, pointing out possible long-range consequences of bad behavior has little impact on shaping the behavior of early adolescents. They are more impressed with the immediate, with the tangible results of actions. The idea of failing a test if they are caught cheating will have more influence than the idea that they may possibly do poorly in college if they cheat rather than study now.

The ideals of an adult, the altruistic vision of morality as expressed in the Beatitudes and by the cross, is still beyond this age group. We should hold up these ideals and lay the foundations for such a moral vision, but it is unrealistic to expect any but the most precocious youth to appreciate that realm of moral insight and motivation. At this stage in development, therefore, we must be satisfied with promoting a practical morality of logic and common sense. Thankfully much of the basic moral teaching of the Church can be justified at this level.

Physical Development. Puberty complicates and intensifies much of what we have already said about this age group. On the strictly chemical level, early adolescents experience hormonal changes that can produce wide mood swings that have no relationship to the situation around them. They can be depressed and listless one minute and giddy and agitated the next.

help matters either. Many youth possess bodies that seem totally disproportionate. Feet and noses may not "fit" the rest of them. They do not yet have good coordination in the newly expanded arms and legs. There can be a natural awkwardness about their appearance and movements that does little to bolster their security and relieve their self-consciousness. The ambivalence early adolescents feel toward themselves is often extended to persons of the other sex. On one hand, boys and girls feel a natural curiosity and attraction toward each other. On the other hand, they prefer the safety and anonymity of a same-sex group where they can solidify their male or female identity.

Because each person has his or her own "body clock" when it comes to experiencing puberty, you can anticipate a wide range of difference in physical development among early adolescents. Girls typically mature physically and emotionally at an earlier age than

Adolescents prefer hands-on activitie and projects that produce tangible results over those that involve abstract discussion, reflection and long-range results.

The broader physical aspects of puberty—the growth spurt, the physical changes in reproductive organs, the strange new sexual stirrings and sensations—do not

boys. This gap is most obvious between seventh and ninth grade. Usually by tenth grade, the boys begin to catch up both physically and emotionally.

Some individuals may be significantly ahead of or behind in development in relation to their peers. This situation can further intensify feelings of self-consciousness. It can also complicate attempts to relate to the opposite sex.

Summary

We should always keep in mind that, regardless of legitimate generalizations about this age group, each person is a unique individual and should be respected as such. Despite the generalizations, there will always be exceptions to the above descriptions. Some individuals may possess a maturity beyond their years and may already begin to manifest a capacity for spiritual insight. Other individuals may move easily into the world of the imaginative and symbolic despite the overall group's propensity to prefer the logical. Others may continue to cling to childlike (or childish) behavior, being in no hurry to seek independence from parents and other authority figures.

Given the uniqueness of each individual, we can still identify the following general traits proper to early adolescents:

- They are two-dimensional, still lacking the capacity for spiritual insight and for adult faith. Logic is their strong suit.
- In terms of personal identity, there is a lot of ambivalence; insecurity and self-consciousness shape much of their behavior.
- Socially, they now depend upon their peer group for approval and acceptance. Given their natural insecurity and self-consciousness, they are very vulnerable to peer pressure.
- Morally, they tend to be legalistic. Moral rules have motivating value only to the degree that they are fair, logical, and immediate.
- Puberty, with its hormonal changes, growth spurts, and the awakening of sexual stirrings, tends to complicate and intensify much of the ambivalence, insecurity, and self-consciousness proper to this age group.

The following information and suggestions can help you formulate your overall approach to teaching the courses of the *Crossroads* program.

T13

Catechetical Philosophy
and goals of *Crossroads*

Rooted in the apostolic tradition

When the apostles began their mission to "teach all nations," they proclaimed a simple message of good news: God has entered into human history in a definitive way through Jesus to save us from the power of sin and everlasting death and to bring us to fullness of life. In the process, they explained how these saving deeds of God were foreshadowed in the Passover events of Jewish history and achieved in the new Passover of Jesus' death and resurrection. Those who accepted this message were first initiated into this Paschal mystery through Baptism and the anointing of the Holy Spirit. Then they began a new life as disciples of Jesus and were gradually schooled in the responsibilities of discipleship through ongoing participation in the life and the worship of the community of disciples.

These core activities of the apostles form the basis for the goals and methods of catechesis employed in the *Crossroads* program.

1. Proclaim and explain the good news of the Paschal mystery.
2. Nurture ongoing understanding of this good news and the discipleship it entails.
3. Develop the skills of discipleship through participation in the life and the worship of the community of disciples.

To fully appreciate the implications of these goals as they apply to a catechesis for youth in the twenty-first century, we need to examine each in more detail.

The good news . . .

At the time when the apostles and first Christians boldly went forth, their message was truly both "good" and "new." They spoke powerfully of a God who was a loving, saving Abba, actively concerned and intimately involved with the plight of each individual person. They spoke of personal resurrection and of eternal life where those who were poor and lowly would reign and feast. This indeed sounded like "good news" to people who were imprisoned in ignorance, injustice, alienation, and hopelessness.

Twenty centuries later, this same good news does not necessarily sound either "good" or "new" to many youth. Some young people are constantly distracted by the kind of "immediate salvation" that science, affluence, and modern technology seem to offer. The rewards promised through a life of faith and discipleship may not seem particularly "good" by comparison. Others, having been exposed to religious instruction from childhood onward, may feel that they have "heard it all before." By high school, the

We need to break through our religious clichés, so that youth can experience the real power and challenge of the gospel, perhaps for the first time.

gospel hardly seems like "news" to them.

The **first goal** and the first challenge of youth catechesis, therefore, is to present the good news in a fresh and simple manner. We need to break through our religious clichés, so that youth can experience the real power and challenge of the gospel, perhaps for the first time. We need to alert youth to the false salvation held out by some elements of our culture so that they can appreciate the radical nature of the justice and salvation the gospel actually proclaims. The *Crossroads* program seeks to do just that, both through the way it presents its content and also through the methods it suggests.

. . . of the Paschal mystery

The concept of the Paschal mystery summarized the revelation contained in the Old Testament,

and it summarizes the work of Jesus recorded in the New Testament. The Paschal mystery was the *kerygma* or "content" of the proclamation and catechesis of the apostolic Church. It remains

our content today. Essentially, we proclaim and teach that our God is a faithful, forgiving, saving God, intimately involved in our history and our plight. No matter how hopeless our situation and regardless of whether it is brought about by our own sinfulness or the injustice of others, God never abandons us. Thus God acted throughout the Old Testament. Thus God the Father acted through Jesus. Thus God continues to act today.

Respecting our freedom, God patiently and gently invites us to reject those idols and false gods by which many hope to be saved (power, fame, wealth, magic,

science, and so forth) and to put our whole faith in his love and his promise (covenant) instead. That is how God invited and taught Abraham and each new generation of Abraham and Sarah's descendants throughout

their entire Old Testament history. That is how Jesus invited and taught the people in his day. The disciples of Jesus were sent to invite and teach all nations in the same way.

The transformation effected by our conversion and consequent faith always exceeds what we expected or even dreamed possible. The children of Abraham and Sarah were snatched out of bondage to the pharaoh, transformed into God's chosen people, and established in the promised land. Jesus was snatched from failure, disgrace, and death and raised up to reign at God the Father's right hand as the Savior and Christ. Each new generation of Jesus' disciples is rescued and radically transformed in turn.

The seasons of the liturgical cycle unfold this Paschal mystery in all its fullness and drama, allowing us to enter into it ever more deeply each year. Each time we gather for Eucharist we recall and re-experience this same Paschal mystery.

It should be clear that the Paschal mystery needs to be the content of our catechetical ministry to youth. Since Vatican II, religious educators have done a good job of updating and deepening our theology, and we have made real strides in adopting psychologically-sound religious education methods. Nevertheless our attempts at catechesis for youth today too often fail because we tend to focus on specific topics and issues before we have shared with the youth the big picture contained in the Paschal mystery. The simple, powerful kerygma of the Paschal mystery needs to be presented in a holistic way.

The **second goal** of catechesis for youth, therefore, is to return to and focus on the simple, powerful integrating kerygma of the Paschal mystery. Youth, eager to find meaning amid a bewildering pluralism of values and philosophies of our day, are hungry for such a holistic, yet simple, message. Because they are in transition to adulthood, they are no longer satisfied with the study of isolated truths, no matter how valid and how important each of those truths is in its own right. Only by presenting this more comprehensive kerygma can we hope to call youth to conversion and to adult faith. The second goal of the *Crossroads* program is to relate each topic presented to this larger, more comprehensive kerygma of the Paschal mystery.

Discipleship

Christian faith is rooted in the person of Jesus Christ. Christian faith means discipleship. It requires a personal entrusting of oneself, not just to a set of moral ideals or even to an institution, but first and foremost to the person of Jesus and through him to the reign of God. This kind of personal, intimate relationship with God was the chief characteristic of Abraham's faith. An intimate friendship with Jesus, Son of God, was the chief

characteristic of the apostles' faith. Each consequent generation of Christians have been called to be disciples, personally committed to Jesus and to the reign of God Jesus proclaimed.

Personal discipleship, however, does not translate into a kind of "me and Jesus" religiosity. Rather, personal discipleship binds us intimately to all other disciples. Discipleship means fellowship and community. God formed the children of Abraham into a people and a nation, destined to be a light to all the nations. Jesus formed his apostles into a community of disciples and sent them forth to be a light to all the world. The apostles, in turn, called all who would listen into this same fellowship of disciples and to the mission of witnessing to the reign of God.

Being and maintaining ourselves as a visible community of disciples with a specific mission requires organization, official teachers and official teachings, common rites and rituals. In short, there is an institutional dimension implied in discipleship and in being a community of disciples.

A tension between community and institution is always possible. There is also a danger, rooted in the effects of original sin, that the institutional aspect of faith and discipleship, being both tangible and immediate, can become an end in itself and actually compete with authentic faith and discipleship. Membership in and

loyalty to the teachings and laws of the institution can be mistaken for discipleship. Maintaining the institution can be mistaken for promoting the reign of God. This tension can be seen in the entire history of the Church, beginning with the apostles (see, for example, the struggle between Peter and Paul over circumcision).

Our own moment in history is not without this tension. Too often our catechesis for youth has been geared to forming them and maintaining them as good members of the institution rather than as disciples whose faith is rooted in a personal relationship with Jesus. We can sometimes get caught up in teaching about the institutional dimensions of our Church while overlooking the object of our faith, the person of Jesus. Clearly our concern here is one of balance. Teaching about the Church as institution and promoting loyal and responsible membership are integral aspects of our catechesis to youth. But these emphases should never overshadow the more fundamental content of Jesus, the call to personal discipleship, and our commitment to the reign of God.

The **third goal** of youth catechesis, therefore, is to foster personal faith in Jesus and discipleship with him. Only when youth are rooted in this personal faith and discipleship will they be able to fully appreciate and respond to our catechesis related to membership in the Church and the implications of that membership.

A dominant theme throughout the *Crossroads* program is the person of Jesus and one's call to personal discipleship.

Community of disciples

For catechesis to be effective, it must be rooted in a community of faith. On the one hand, as we just described, community is the goal of catechesis. God patiently formed the Hebrews into a

chosen people. Jesus patiently formed his disciples into a community, as new people of God. Each new generation of disciples, from the apostles onward, call, initiate, and form converts into a community of disciples.

On the other hand and more to the point here, the community of disciples plays an essential role in providing the ongoing witness and support necessary to nurture and maintain personal faith and discipleship. Just as important, the liturgical life of the faith and community, wherein the Pascal mystery is continually re-presented and celebrated, is critical to the faith development of the individual. It is by such immersion in the interaction with the community of disciples that new disciples best learn the skills and practices necessary to integrate their faith. When such witness, support, and vital liturgy is

missing—when catechesis takes place within a vacuum—all efforts at individual catechesis are seriously impaired.

The adult catechumenate, re-established throughout the Church, clearly recognizes this principle. The witness, support, and worship of a visible faith community is considered essential to the overall process of the faith development of these adult converts. For the catechesis of children and youth, faith community has always meant not just the local parish community but also—and more important in many ways—the immediate family or household in which they live. Each household, ideally, is to function as a domestic Church, a community of disciples in miniature.

When the witness of the local parish and the household is strong, the work of the youth catechist is relatively easy. But being realistic, much catechesis for youth takes place today in a kind of vacuum. For various reasons too numerous to describe here, many parishes and many households are not providing the kind of witness, support, and liturgical celebration we would like. This seriously impairs the effectiveness of youth catechesis, regardless of how

good the religious education texts may be and how well the religious education programs are designed.

The **fourth goal** of youth catechesis, therefore, is to provide ongoing opportunities for youth to experience and become involved in the life and work of the local faith community. Even though the witness of the adult faith community and the family may not always be what we would hope, it remains essential that we recognize the importance of this witness and continue to do all we can to integrate youth into the life and worship of the local faith community. The *Crossroads* program is committed to this goal in principle and seeks to facilitate such involvement in practice.

Summary

The *Crossroads* program is developed around the following underlying goals, which permeate and shape the individual texts and all other components of the program.

Crossroads seeks:
• to focus on the integrating kerygma of the Paschal mystery;
• to present this good news in a simple, fresh manner designed to appeal to youth in today's culture;
• to call youth to personal faith in Jesus and discipleship with him;
• to encourage and, when possible, to provide ongoing opportunities for youth to experience and become involved in the life and worship of the local faith community.

CROSS✦ROADS

Content and Curriculum Models for *Crossroads*

Core curriculum and electives

There are nine basic, eight-session courses in the *Crossroads* program:

- Apostles' Creed
- Church History
- Commandments
- Discipleship
- Jesus in the New Testament
- Morality
- Old Testament
- Prayer
- Sacraments

Electives, in the form of mini-courses or full courses can be added to this core curriculum. For example, the sixth, seventh, and eighth grade texts of a human sexuality program (BROWN-ROA's, for example) generally fit nicely into the program for this age group, in both format and philosophy. A Confirmation program (BROWN–ROA's, again as an example) can be easily integrated into your junior high program. Confirmation programs usually reflect and build on the themes of Paschal mystery and discipleship developed in the basic texts of the *Crossroads* program. *Crossroads* works best when it is used within a ministry framework. When looking at the entire year, every effort should be made to offer ministry opportunities: service, liturgical, and social.

Sequencing the curriculum

There is an inherent logical order suggested by some of the topics. For example, it makes sense to present the life of Jesus before studying the history of the Church and the sacraments. Nevertheless, since each course is designed to be self-contained, and a unifying theology and catechetical philosophy runs through all courses in the core curriculum, it is possible to mix and match as you see fit. You are not bound to any particular order. This gives you great flexibility, and you can develop your program to suit your circumstances. Here is a sample model that illustrates this flexibility.

Three-Year Program
Year One: Old Testament, Commandments, Prayer
Year Two: Jesus in the New Testament, Sacraments, Discipleship
Year Three: Morality, Church History, Apostles' Creed

Two-Year Program
Year One: Jesus in the New Testament, Apostles' Creed, Sacraments
Year Two: Church History, Morality, Discipleship

Also, because you are not bound to any particular order, you have flexibility in how you structure your program. If your classes are small, for example, you can combine two or three grades into one class and use a cycle approach, alternating the two-year program or three-year program from above.

Some catechists prefer to use a modified elective format. This works well if you have a large number of students in each grade. In this format, offer each course at a given grade level two or three times during the year. Allow youth a certain amount of freedom in deciding the order in which they take these courses. An added bonus in this format is that you can ask your catechists to serve as experts in a particular course, which becomes their specialty. They teach only this course, but are asked to teach it two or three times during the year.

You have virtually limitless possibilities to design your program to suit your circumstances, class size, and the availability of teachers.

It should be clear that you have virtually limitless possibilities to design your program to suit your circumstances, class size, and the availability of teachers. As you review the student texts and become familiar with their content, you will be able to decide the best sequence for your purposes and program design. When we discuss scheduling options, you will also be able to integrate opportunities for providing other youth ministry experiences without sacrificing the content of the core curriculum.

Planning the Course
and the lessons

The following information and suggestions can help you formulate your overall approach to teaching the courses of the *Crossroads* program.

The student text

The student text consists of the following components:

Eight chapters. The body of the text is divided into brief, titled sections. You can use these titles when referring students to a particular area in the chapter. The text presents essential age-appropriate material related to the topic. NOTE: What has been judged essential is admittedly arbitrary. It is not easy to condense a two thousand-year-old tradition into a few short pages. If information is omitted that you feel should be introduced, by all means do so. But be assured that what is covered in the text is adequate for this age group and can be considered core information.

Information boxes. These shaded areas found throughout the text contain bits of information concerning the chapter. Some of this information is "trivia," designed to entertain and pique the curiosity of students. Some of this information contains useful additional information relating to the topic at hand. You can often use this material as a basis for introducing topics you consider important that are not covered in the body of the chapter.

Group activities. Because peer relationships are an important part of life for early adolescents, the *Crossroads* books emphasize peer learning through group activities. These activities may include artwork, crafts, group discussions, Scripture searches, or prayer.

Journal entries. Throughout the text, students are encouraged to reflect and to write down their personal responses to the subject being studied. Never ask them to share with the class what they have written in a journal entry. The catechist or teacher, however, should periodically collect the students' textbooks and journals to make sure the students are completing the journal activities. The catechist or teacher should also scan for indications of problems that should be addressed.

Scripture searches. These activities, done either in small groups or by individuals, encourage hands-on use of the Bible. Students will become familiar with particular Scripture passages and will gain proficiency in locating these passages in the Bible. Furthermore, students will be challenged to reflect on the message of the Scripture passage and to apply this message to their own lives.

Reflections. These basic outlines give students a structure for reflecting on the chapter and for praying. Both individual and group reflections are provided.

Homework. Each chapter ends with an activity that students are encouraged to complete with their families at home. This aspect of the lesson encourages the involvement of parent(s)/guardian(s) as the students review the chapter and complete the assignment.

Here are a few suggestions to consider in preparing for the course:
- Read through the entire chapter before you plan your class. This will give you a good feel for the flow, overall development, and scope of the chapter.
- Underline points that strike you and that you may wish to stress.
- In the margin, note any sections where you may wish to expand on the concept presented. If you feel unfamiliar with a

particular topic and need more background, note that as well.

• Gather any materials the students may need throughout the course of the class.

Homework

An essential feature of the *Crossroads* program is the requirement that students review the chapter with their families and do a certain amount of additional homework. The program director can facilitate this process by holding a parent meeting prior to the beginning of the program. At this meeting, the necessity and rationale of homework can be explained. It is important that students complete their chapter reviews and homework assignments. They will be tested on each chapter at the beginning of the next class. Their homework assignments will be graded. These scores, along with the student's active participation in the class, will determine the student's grade for the course.

If you do alter the assignments in the text, be sure to prepare a handout to be given to the parents.

NOTE: Always return homework assignments and quizzes to the students with a grade or some appropriate comments on them. If assignments and quizzes are not returned, students will begin to feel that they are busywork and will not take them seriously.

If particular students are not doing their homework, call their parent(s)/guardian(s). Sometimes one phone call is all it takes to effect cooperation of the parent(s)/guardian(s) and youth. The earlier you do this in the course, the better.

An essential feature of the *Crossroads* program is the requirement that the students review the chapter with their families.

Testing

It is a proven fact that students this age perform better and actually enjoy a course more when they are held accountable and, at the same time, experience some sense of mastery or accomplishment. For this reason, it is important that the students be quizzed regularly and that there be some form of final test at the end of the course.

A regular routine of using a quiz to begin each session starts the class in an orderly, businesslike manner. Students will be in their seats on time and be ready to work if this routine is established. Starting with a simple quiz helps focus the students' attention on what they have already learned. It underscores the expectation that they come prepared to class, having reviewed the material and having completed the homework.

You are free, of course, to quiz only as much as you personally feel is necessary. Some days you may prefer to begin the class with oral questions; other days, you may prefer to begin with a written quiz. You may choose, on occasion, to substitute a written assignment for a quiz. In any event, there should be some routine quizzing throughout the course. The final test need not be lengthy, but it should be used to complete the course.

We are asking you to keep student records and to provide some form of grade at the end of each course. Assuming your class is relatively small, this is not as great a burden as it may first appear.

Sufficient optional activities are identified in the lesson procedure to expand the lesson if necessary.

The overall effect it has on the attitude and the learning of the students will be worth the extra effort it requires of you. If answers are brief and factual, it is often possible to have students exchange papers and correct the quizzes in class. This procedure gives you a chance to review the material before beginning the new lesson.

It is usually a good idea to take the major portion of the final test from the questions at the end of the chapters. You may wish to identify two or three questions from each chapter as those the students should focus on in preparing for the test. This way, you can highlight the material you definitely want the students to know, and it takes some of the anxiety out of student preparation. Also consider including at least one thought question in the final test.

Thought questions can be a good way to gain some insight into the students' attitudes toward the topic.

If time is limited and you don't want to spend class time on a final test, it is always possible to give an "open book" test as a written assignment to be done at home. This practice ensures that the students review the material one last time before moving on to another course. It also gives you an opportunity to highlight the concepts you consider important.

Lesson plans

Each course of the *Crossroads* program is accompanied by a set of eight lesson plans, one for each chapter in the student text. The format of these lesson plans is the same throughout and consists of the following:
- Lesson goals
- Procedures (including optional activities)
- Resource Center
- Teacher background information
- Additional teacher resources
- Materials needed
- Audiovisual options
- Chapter quiz

Each lesson is designed with flexibility in mind, either for one session of approximately sixty to ninety minutes (which is the average length of a parish religious education session throughout the country) or for shorter sessions throughout the week, as in a Catholic school. Sufficient optional activities are identified in the lesson procedure to expand the lesson if necessary. The lesson can be taught in a condensed form in about forty-five minutes. However, to cut the lesson to less than forty-five minutes is not advisable. It would be better to cover a chapter in two sessions if your sessions are less than forty-five minutes. Here are some suggestions to consider when planning each lesson:

- Before class, read the chapter of the student text to familiarize yourself with what it contains. Note concepts and information you wish to add to this material, as well as concepts you wish to stress.
- Read the Resource Center at the bottom of the lesson plan pages. If you need additional background, it will be included here. This section provides additional information and insights that correlate to the student text. It is not necessary to teach the material, but it does give you a broader base from which to work when you are teaching the material in the text.
- Note any pre-class preparation or materials that are required.
- Read over the entire procedure outlined in the lesson plan. Note that various steps in the procedure are sometimes followed by alternative and/or optional activities.
- Reread the procedure and decide exactly which of the various steps you will follow and which options or alternatives you will use. Don't hesitate to eliminate a step or an activity with which you feel uncomfortable. Don't hesitate to substitute an activity of your own that you feel might be better than the one suggested. (The procedure outlined is a suggested approach using proven activities. But it need not be followed strictly. It provides the basic materials from which you can construct your own personalized lesson plan. The more comfortable you feel with the lesson plan, as tailored by you, the more effective you will be at teaching it.)
- If you decide to use any of the audiovisual materials identified, be sure to plan ahead to have the necessary equipment for viewing. If possible, always preview audiovisual material before showing it to the students.
- Review your entire lesson plan as edited and constructed by you. Walk through each step mentally to ensure that you know just what you should do and how you will move from one step to the next. This mental rehearsal is an invaluable aid in preparation.
- Finally, proceed to gather any necessary materials you will need, based on the edited lesson plan you have constructed.

Teaching Methods

Introduction

Many books have been written on how people learn and what is involved in good teaching. At the risk of oversimplifying, we can reduce the educational process to three basic kinds of activities: information gathering, interpretation, and application.

Information gathering means that data is collected from personal experience and observation or from what others tell us of their own personal experience and observations. The infant gathers information by touching, handling, tasting, and looking. Small children gather information in much the same way, but also benefit by the experience and observation of others. They gather information by sitting on Grandpa's lap and hearing him recount his tales of the "good old days." Others tell them two plus two equals four. Scientists gather information through complex, controlled experiments. Pollsters gather information through interviews and questionnaires. Information gathering satisfies our innate need for knowledge and provides a basis for deeper understanding and for informed action.

Interpretation means that one seeks or discovers a pattern in what, at first, appears to be a series of unrelated facts. From that pattern, one draws a conclusion, a law, a generalization. A law or generalization is a way of expressing some truth about reality. The ability to arrive at laws or principles by means of analyzing or interpreting a collection of facts is the next step in education.

Application is when one learns to take the laws and principles derived from interpretation and apply them to other actual or possible situations. For example, students in music are asked to read the biographies of famous musicians. This activity is data gathering. In reflecting on what they read, the students observe that all the successful musicians had natural talent and put in long hours of practice to develop their art. That is interpretation. Some students decide they do not wish to pursue a career in music because they lack either the natural talent or are unwilling to devote long hours to practice. That is application. The students have made an educated decision.

Obviously our goal in religious education follows the same structure. (1) We seek to help the students gather information found in their own experience and in the experiences of their ancestors in faith (information gathering). (2) We seek to help students learn how to reflect upon and interpret that information (truths of the faith) so that it becomes the students' own beliefs (interpretation). (3) We hope to guide and motivate students to apply these truths to their own lives and to use them in arriving at their own personal decisions (application).

Any method that focuses solely on acquiring information is clearly defective religious education. (Yet it must be observed that at certain stages in a child's development, more time is properly spent on this aspect of education than on the other two. The need for information is especially strong in the very young, who do not yet have fully-developed powers of interpretation and application. We must still help them interpret and apply this information.) By early adolescence, students have reached the stage in their intellectual development where it is possible—and advisable—to provide a good balance of all three dimensions of the educational process. The lesson plans in this guide seek to provide that kind of balance. What follows is a collection of various teaching methods, strategies, suggestions, and tips

those facts necessary to what they are studying. This questioning includes the who, what, when, where, why, and how.

Interpretation. Interpretative questioning helps students reflect upon the data they have gathered in order to recognize any patterns or generalizations. This kind of questioning usually focuses on the meaning and purpose of things. "Why do you think the apostles decided . . . ?" "How would you explain why the apostles decided . . . ?" "What do you think is the relationship between . . . ?"

Application. In this form of questioning, you direct the students to think about the

The need for information is especially strong in the very young, who do not yet have fully-developed powers of interpretation and application.

related to the three dimensions of the educational process.

Questioning

One of the oldest teaching methods is the art of questioning. Jesus frequently used this method during his ministry. The secret to this art is knowing why you are asking questions. Questions can be used as a means to help students collect and organize facts. They can be used to help students interpret the facts gathered. Or they can be used to help students begin to apply these interpretations to their own lives. Each purpose has its own form of questioning.

Facts. Factual questioning should relate information to the students' personal experience. Personal experience is the most influential form of fact gathering. Equally important, the information others share with us takes on more value if we can associate it with our own personal experience. That's why questions such as "Did you ever feel . . . ?" or "Did you ever meet a person who . . . ?" or "How many times have you . . . ?" help students analyze data from their own life experiences.

Here, one of the more obvious purposes of questioning is simply to see if the students have grasped

material learned in terms of their own lives. "What do you think you would do if . . . ?" "What could you do this week to follow Jesus' teaching on . . . ?" "How would you feel if . . . ?" In this kind of questioning, it is good to involve as many students as possible, to demonstrate that there are many possible ways to apply a principle to one's life.

Brainstorming

To initiate a brainstorming session, ask the class a question such as "What do you think of when you hear the words ,'Ten Commandments'?" Students then give their spontaneous responses, which are written on the chalkboard. After a sufficient number of responses, the next step is to look for common patterns. You may look for two general categories of responses, negative ones and positive ones, for example, and group them as such.

This same method can be used for problem-solving activities. The one basic rule in brainstorming is that each student's response be accepted in a nonjudgmental way. Otherwise students will be hesitant to participate, and the process breaks down.

Gaming

By "gaming" we mean the use of familiar game structures (for example, TV quiz shows, baseball, "Twenty Questions") as a framework for an activity. Students can form groups to compete against one another, or they can work as teams to prepare questions to be asked of opponents.

Role-playing

In using this familiar activity, it is good to observe several rules with this age group:
- Involve groups of students in the activity. One-on-one role-playing does not work as well with students this age.
- Choose situations within the students' range of experiences. Playing a situation in which one group tries to convince another group that smoking is cool is realistic.
- Maintain audience participation among the students not

involved in the role-playing by asking them to serve as judges. They should be prepared to make a decision regarding the authenticity of the words and actions of the role-players, and they should be prepared to explain why they felt the players were believable or not believable in their roles.

Group work

In almost every lesson, there are suggested group activities. Students this age enjoy and can work effectively in groups. It is one of the better teaching methods for them. The following suggestions may help you utilize this method.

Group size and makeup

For students of this age, a group of no more than five or six is best.

If the group is too large, some students are forced to the fringes of the activity, and this can lead to discipline problems. Typically, students will work best if the groups are segregated according to gender. This capitalizes on a natural competitiveness between the sexes proper to this age. It also minimizes the self-consciousness common between the sexes at this age. However, it is always possible to mix boys and girls in the same group, especially if the class is small and the students have developed a wholesome class rapport. If you do form mixed groups of boys and girls, try to have an equal number of boys and girls in each group.

Group situations

At this age, students enjoy group situations and can work well in

Students this age can enjoy and work effectively in groups.

them, provided you follow a few simple rules:

- Be sure to give each group a very clear task. Stress accountability. That is, at the end of a certain time, you will expect some "result" from the group's work.
- Give a definite time limit so that students know precisely how long they have for the task. Stress the "team" concept, in which all feel some responsibility for the work of the group.
- Groups can be used for a variety of educational activities. Activities such as reviewing, problem-solving, prioritizing, and planning lend themselves to small-group work. Most of the activities that are suggested in the lesson plans can be done in a group structure.

Caution: This age group does not handle group discussion well in its pure, abstract form. That is, you cannot ask the groups to discuss a vague topic, such as "the role of

covenant in your lives." Effective discussion with students this age must always be specific. For example, "See if your group can come up with five different kinds of covenants you are involved in today."

Group duration

It is a good idea to keep a group together for several weeks before forming new groups. This technique allows students enough time to develop a team spirit and to experience some successes together. You may want to have each group give itself a name when it is first formed. For example, a group might adopt its name from one of the New Testament books (Ephesians, Corinthians, and so forth). Another time a group might choose a name or be assigned a name from the disciples (for example, Peter's Panthers, Lydia's Lions, John's Jets).

Forming groups

To minimize confusion and potential discipline problems, establish a clear routine for gathering into groups. For example, group A always forms first in the back left-hand corner of the room; then group B forms in the right-hand corner, and so forth. Follow the same routine each time. After several classes, you will be able to form the groups quickly and without any confusion.

Pairs and trios

Some activities suggest that you form students into pairs or threesomes. Depending on the nature of the activity, you may want to respect the principle of

separating the genders. However, such activities are often of shorter duration, and pairs can be formed "ad hoc." For example, pairs can be formed by the two students sitting across from each other.

Audiovisual materials

At the end of each chapter's lesson plan is a section listing various audiovisual resources related to the topic of the chapter. These lists are not intended to be exhaustive; new materials are being developed regularly. The lesson plans never include the use of audiovisuals, not because they are not an important teaching tool, but because we did not want any lesson plan to be dependent upon the availability of the audiovisuals.

If you do have access to the materials identified or to any others suitable for the chapter under study, don't hesitate to include them in your lesson. Simply eliminate one of the other suggested activities dealing with the same information. Students of this age are very visually oriented, so we do encourage you to use suitable audiovisuals when they are available to you. However, keep in mind the standard caution in this regard: Never use an audiovisual unless you have a clear teaching objective in mind. Then follow the audiovisual with a suitable learning activity, such as a discussion or application exercise. Audiovisuals can enhance good teaching, but cannot be used as a substitute for a well-prepared lesson.

Course Overview

The course *Crossroads Morality* has two main goals—one academic and the other attitudinal.

Academic Goal: To understand the nature of morality, its rational foundations, and the new dimensions that faith gives to those foundations.

Attitudinal Goal: To experience, in a positive light, the moral challenge presented by the gospel as a call to full humanness and to accept this challenge as both desirable and possible.

Course summary

Human morality begins with rationality—what's reasonable. Such rationality may be summed up in the Golden Rule. Christian morality, however, goes a step further. Our faith in Jesus gives us "new eyes" for understanding basic morality. Jesus doesn't give us new "rules." He gives us an entirely new appreciation of our own dignity and the dignity of our neighbor. Consequently, the following fundamental theme runs through the entire course: Authentic Christian morality is rooted in our ability to see and love ourselves the way Jesus sees and loves us. The nature of conscience is explained in this context. Every person, because of different family and environmental influences, tends to have a "personalized" conscience. As we mature, we continually need to refine our "personalized" conscience. The text presents practical steps for how to do this.

The text describes the nature and limits of human freedom, together with the nature and limits of human responsibility. The point is made that faith increases our moral freedom, but also increases our moral responsibility.

Students learn that, throughout life, they will encounter three types of moral decisions— everyday decisions, snap decisions, and big decisions. The text presents suggestions for approaching each type of decision. Emphasis is placed on the everyday decisions because they play the biggest part in determining the kind of person we will ultimately end up becoming (choosing to be).

The last chapter discusses the role of the Church as a moral guide and companion throughout our moral journey. Students will see the importance of the Sacrament of Reconciliation, especially for the times when they fail to make good moral decisions.

Throughout the course, other topics are also discussed—the nature and role of natural moral law, the difference between freedom and liberty, the distinction between objective and subjective guilt, the Church's understanding of mortal sin, and the elements for repentance and conversion. Students are challenged to assume an adult approach to and accept responsibility for their own moral development.

Course materials

Throughout this course, you will need the following materials:
- Bibles
- chalkboard and chalk
- pens/pencils
- music for prayer

If any other materials are needed, they will be listed throughout the chapter.

THE
CROSS ROADS
SERIES

MORALITY

Author
Richard J. Reichert

BROWN-ROA
A Division of Harcourt Brace & Company

About the author of the student text

Richard Reichert has a master's degree in religious education from Loyola University of Chicago. For the past twenty years, he has been a consultant for youth and adult catechsis in the diocese of Green Bay. He is not only the author of over thirty religious education textbooks and monographs, but has played a significant role in the development of both the National Catechetical Directory (*Sharing the Light of Faith*) and the basic guidelines for Catholic educators, *To Teach as Jesus Did*. Additionally, Mr. Reichert has served on several bishops' committees for the development of guidelines in the areas of sexuality education and morality.

BROWN-ROA
A Division of Harcourt Brace & Company

Our Mission

The primary mission of BROWN-ROA is to provide the
Catholic and Christian educational markets with the
highest quality catechetical print and media resources.
The content of these resources reflects the best insights
of current theology, methodology, and pedagogical research.
The resources are practical and easy to use, designed to meet
expressed market needs, and written to reflect the
teachings of the Catholic Church.

Nihil Obstat
Rev. Richard L. Schaefer

Imprimatur
✠ Most Rev. Jerome Hanus, O.S.B.
Archbishop of Dubuque
January 4, 1998
Feast of Saint Elizabeth Ann Seton

The Imprimatur is an official declaration that a book or pamphlet is free of doctrinal or moral error.
No implication is contained therein that anyone who granted the Imprimatur agrees with the
contents, opinions, or statements expressed.

Copyright © 1999 by BROWN-ROA, a division of Harcourt Brace & Company

All rights reserved. No part of this publication may be reproduced or transmitted in any form or by
any means, electronic or mechanical, including photocopy, recording, or any information storage and
retrieval system, without permission in writing from the publisher.

Requests for permission to make copies of any part of the work should be mailed to the following
address: Permissions Department, Harcourt Brace & Company, 6277 Sea Harbor Drive, Orlando,
Florida 32887-6777.

Portions of this work were published in previous editions.

Excerpts from the English translation of the *Catechism of the Catholic Church* for use in the United
States of America Copyright © 1994, United States Catholic Conference, Inc.—Libreria Editrice
Vaticana. Used with Permission.

The Scripture quotations contained herein are from the New Revised Standard Version Bible: Catholic
Edition copyright © 1993 and 1989 by the Division of Christian Education of the National Council of
the Churches of Christ in the U.S.A. Used by permission. All rights reserved.

Illustrations—Rob Suggs

Photo Credits: Nancy Anne Dawe—57; Robert Fried—16, 32, 41, 45; Robert Cushman Hayes—24, 35,
51; Mary Messenger—14; Robert Roethig—22, 30; James L. Shaffer—2, 7, 8, 37, 42, 61, 67, 79, 81, 85, 86,
90; Skjold Photography—68; D. Jeanene Tiner—20, 50, 52; Jim Whitmer—10, 12, 63

Printed in the United States of America

ISBN 0-15-950466-X

10 9 8 7 6 5 4 3 2 1

What's Coming

iii

At the first class meeting . . .

1. Introduce yourself to the students if this is a new group. Tell them a few facts about yourself, some of your interests, and your reason for teaching this class.

2. Distribute the *Morality* textbooks to the students. Allow the students time to look through the books.

Introductory Activities

1. Direct the students' attention to **Who will you be?** activity on page **iv**. Make available the needed materials.

2. Read aloud the directions, one by one, as the students follow them.

3. Write the following "formula" on the chalkboard. Then have the students take turns filling in the blanks with the answers they have on the paper before them.

Formula

My name is _____.

I plan on becoming an adult by the time I am (section 1).

By then I hope to be a (section 2).

This career will make me (section 3) and will make others (section 3).

I got to this point in life because I (section 4) my homework and (section 4) my parents.

4. When all the students have read from their papers, have them individually complete the questions in the **Who are you now?** section on page **iv**.

5. For the one-on-one sharing, encourage the students to pair with someone they don't know very well. You may want to help the process along by pairing boys with boys and girls with girls.

6. Gather all the students in one group and invite them to take turns introducing one another.

Materials
- sheets of paper

Who will you be?

How do your present choices shape the person you will be in the future? Play this game to find out. (For each person in the group, you'll need paper and a pen or pencil.)

Directions

1. Fold the paper like an accordion into four sections. Starting with the top section, label the sections 1, 2, 3, and 4.

2. In section 1, write down a number between 16 and 90. Then fold the paper so that only section 2 is visible. Pass the paper to the person on your right.

3. In section 2, write down a noun (a person, place, or thing, such as dog, girl, pumpkin, house, etc.). Then fold the paper so that only section 3 is visible. Pass the paper to the person on your right.

4. In section 3, write down two adjectives (hungry, happy, sleepy, etc.). Then fold the paper so that only section 4 is visible. Pass the paper to the person on your right.

5. In section 4, write down two verbs in the past tense (ran, saw, jumped, etc.). Pass the paper to the person on your right.

6. Take turns reading aloud the papers according to the formula your teacher will give you.

Who are you now?

For each example, underline the choice that best expresses who you are right now.

If I could choose anything for dessert, I'd choose: (A) apple pie, (B) chocolate cake, (C) an ice cream sundae, (D) a candy bar.

If I could buy a new CD, it'd be: (A) classical, (B) rock, (C) rap, (D) country.

If I could do anything this weekend, I would: (A) play soccer, (B) watch TV, (C) hang out at the mall, (D) go for a hike.

If I could pick out an outfit that's "me," I'd pick something: (A) dressy, (B) sporty, (C) comfortable, (D) fashionable.

If I could have an exotic pet, I'd choose a: (A) snake, (B) pot-bellied pig, (C) homing pigeon, (D) tarantula.

Share your choices with one other person. Ask that person to share his or her choices with you. Then take turns introducing one another to the group.

iv

① Discuss morality.

What's Right? What's Wrong?

Natural law ②

Morality is the study of what's right and what's wrong. Morality is the way we put our beliefs into action for what is good. As you begin this course, it's important to know that morality is not something adults have made up to make teenagers and children miserable. Nor is morality something the Church or the government has dreamed up to keep members or citizens in line. Instead, morality is based on God's revelation and nature itself.

Just think about it for a minute. Water doesn't flow up. It's okay to kill animals to feed humans, but it isn't okay to kill humans to feed animals. Hammers work better for pounding nails than for eating soup. Soap is fine for washing your face, but it doesn't taste too good in a salad.

We discover these basic "laws" by observing, by trial and error, and by using common sense. Certain things have reasonable purposes and limits just by their nature. We call these reasonable

purposes and limits the "natural law" of things. No senate, bishop, or ruler made up the natural law. It has its roots in God's plan for all creation.

To the extent that we can discover the nature (purpose and limits) of anything, we are expected to follow that "law." Not to do so is, for the most part, just plain stupid. In many cases, not to obey the natural law is also immoral because of the harm that results. We are always discovering more about nature and the natural law.

The natural law has always played a big role in trying to decide what is morally right and wrong. In this case we're talking about the natural *moral* law. The objective norms of morality are based on the natural moral law. That is, certain things are by their nature right or wrong. It isn't always as easy as it may seem to know and to apply the natural moral law. But, in general, it's safe to say "It's not nice to fool Mother Nature, and it's often immoral to try."

---

③ "It's Not Nice to Fool Mother Nature"

Choose one of the following topics and then create your own bumper sticker slogan.
- Clean water
- Clean air
- Conserving energy
- Recycling
- Saving an endangered species (which one?)
- Saving the rainforest
- Protecting farmland
- Anti-littering

Write your slogan here:

_____

_____

④ F.Y.I.

Some things we thought were unnatural in ancient times aren't unnatural today. Our ancestors would have thought it was unnatural, for example, to transplant organs from a dead person to a living person. To try it then would have been considered immoral, but now such transplants are considered moral. This is an example of how our understanding of the natural law can change.

1

Resource Center

Teaching Tip

Clarifying concepts: Tell the students that we do not always know how best to put natural moral law into practice. In these situations we look to the Church, which has the responsibility to announce the saving truth of the gospel. The pope and bishops, in consultation with theologians (those who study God's relationship with the world), help us apply the Ten Commandments and Beatitudes to our lives.

The Language of Faith

As creatures endowed with reason, we are able to perceive the *natural moral law*, the moral order of human nature. But because we are sinful, we do not always clearly and immediately perceive what is right. For this reason God made a *covenant*, or sacred agreement, with the people of Israel. It spelled out, through the Ten Commandments, and other laws, how we are to love God and our neighbor.

Lesson Procedure

Academic Goals: To recognize that the basis for determining right and wrong is rooted in God's revelation and nature itself and that the Golden Rule summarizes morality at the level of reason and logic.

Attitudinal Goal: To appreciate that morality is not some arbitrary set of rules but flows from our own experience of how we would like to be treated.

1. Write the word *morality* on the chalkboard, and ask the students to brainstorm words that come to mind when they hear the word *morality*. Write their responses on the board. Then ask the students to look over the list for items they strongly agree or disagree with. Discuss briefly.

2. Have the students take turns reading aloud the text on page **1**. Ask the students for additional examples of the natural law.

3. Have the students work alone to complete the **"It's Not Nice to Fool Mother Nature"** activity.

Optional

Divide the class into eight groups. Assign each group one of the topics listed in the activity. Allow time for the groups to make a poster that illustrates an appropriate bumper sticker slogan. When everyone is finished, call on the groups to share their poster with the class.

4. Be sure to have the students notice the **F.Y.I.** material. These sections throughout the text provide students with interesting "extras."

Materials

- art supplies (optional)

1. Allow time for the students to work individually to write their answers to **How does it feel?** Form groups of three or four for sharing.

 2. Conduct a whole-class discussion of the **Something to talk about** questions.

Optional

Because the natural law is written and engraved in the soul of every person to help discern by reason the good and the evil, people who have never followed the Christian religion often live by the natural law. Have students give examples of Native American customs that carry out the natural law, for example, reverence for creation, respect for courage, and self-sacrifice.

---

① How does it feel?

Morality also has its basis in the natural feelings people have. Complete this page to discover the connection between morality and feelings.

Imagine that you and your friends are playing—perhaps in the park or maybe at the school playground after classes. Some older kids come along and mess up your game or take away your basketball. Or maybe they decide they want your play area. Or maybe they just stand around getting in the way and teasing you.

How does it feel to be teased and bullied?

_____

_____

Has a friend ever lied to you? Suppose you ask a friend to go to the movies with you on Friday night. Your friend says that he or she has to baby-sit and can't go. Later you find out your friend went to another movie with other classmates.

How does it feel when someone important lies to you?

_____

_____

Have you ever been ripped off or had something important to you vandalized? Perhaps you came out of school and found that your bike was gone or that the air had been let out of the tires. Maybe someone deliberately messed up a school project you had worked very hard to complete. Or maybe a brother or sister ruined your favorite sweatshirt.

How does it feel to have your belongings ripped off or vandalized?

_____

_____

Share your answers in small groups.

② SOMETHING TO TALK ABOUT
1. What's wrong in each of the above situations?
2. What does your feeling in each case tell you about the rightness or wrongness of the action?

2

Resource Center

Link to Justice

Many people—such as those who have physical or mental disabilities, those who are over- or underweight or mentally ill, and others—suffer discrimination because of their "unattractive" appearance or "odd" behavior. Stress that as Christians we are called by God to respect *all* people and treat them with dignity. Ask the students to suggest ways to make others feel welcomed and valued.

When people move to a new neighborhood or enroll in a new school, they are sometimes not welcomed and are ignored or teased. Ask the students whether they have ever witnessed or experienced this; invite examples of what was done or not done. Encourage the students to suggest how newcomers should be treated.

Human rights

If you've ever been in one of the situations described on the previous page, you know that you've been wronged. You don't have to find out about it in a book. Even as a small child you knew you had certain rights—the right to play with a friend, to the truth, and to a certain amount of property. Even as a small child you knew it was wrong if people bullied you, lied to you, or stole from you. Because you are human, you have certain rights. You need these rights protected in order to function and to be happy.

Morality is really that simple. You can go anywhere in the world—or go as far back in the history of humanity as you can reach—and find the same fact: Each of us, simply by being human and a child of God, has rights. Everyone knows it's wrong if others violate those rights.

As Christians, morality flows from our personal relationship with Christ. We strive to be good because of God's love for us and our love for God. Our sense morality helps us name certain acts as wrong because those acts violate God's law and our rights as humans.

F.Y.I.

Morality comes from the Latin word *mores*. It means "group customs" or "rules." To be "immoral" means to go against the group's customs or rules. To be "moral" means to follow the group's customs or rules.

Catechism Connection

The natural law is a participation in God's wisdom and goodness . . . It expresses the dignity of the human person and forms the basis of his fundamental rights and duties. (1978)

Form a group with two other people. Together, make a list of rights that you believe belong to all students your age. (Remember, the rights have to follow the natural moral law, respect human dignity, and be reasonable.) When you've finished, share your list with the class.

Rights Belonging to All Students

_____
_____
_____
_____
_____
_____
_____
_____
_____
_____
_____
_____
_____
_____

3

---

3. Ask two students to take turns reading aloud **Human Rights** on page **3**.

4. Ask another student to read aloud the **F.Y.I.** section. Ask the students if they agree or disagree with the statement. Are the group's customs or rules always moral? Is it always immoral to go against the group's customs or rules? Ask the students to explain their answers.

5. Read aloud the **Catechism Connection**. Explain to the students that this quote was taken from the *Catechism for the Catholic Church* and states part of what Catholics believe about morality and human rights.

6. Have the students form groups of three. Allow time for the groups to complete the activity. Invite each group to share with the class its list of rights.

Optional

If time permits, make a whole-class list of rights that all students agree upon. Put these rights on the chalkboard or display them on a bulletin board.

Link to Justice

Discuss with the students the importance of civil law in protecting the dignity and rights of every person. Ask them to name rights that every person should have because they are created in the image and likeness of God. List them on the chalkboard.

Link to Social Studies

Ask the students: What kinds of political or social structures violate human rights? (For example, sweatshops that produce expensive items for wealthier nations, slavery in United States history, discrimination in all forms, and so forth.)

1. Ask volunteers to take turns reading aloud **How God sees justice** on page **4**.

   - What rights do all of us have as children of God, created in his image and likeness? *(right to respect and freedom, right to the necessities for sustaining our lives in dignity, and so forth)*

   - What is different about each of us? *(talents, abilities, intelligence, wealth, physical strength, and so forth)*

   - What does morality take into account? *(rights and responsibilities)*

Optional

Have the students return to their small groups from the **Rights Belonging to All Students** activity on the previous page. Ask each group to create a situation (tell a story) in which the rights of two or more people are in some conflict. The story should include a solution that respects the rights of everyone, even if some compromising must be done. Call on each group to present its situation and solution. Discuss as needed.

Optional

Have each student write the word *justice* vertically on a sheet of paper, one letter per line. Direct the students, either individually or in pairs, to write seven-line poems about becoming the best persons they can be, with the first word of each line starting with the corresponding letter of the word *justice*. When the students have finished, invite volunteers to read their poems aloud.

How God sees justice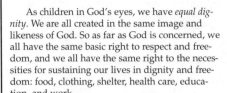

As children in God's eyes, we have *equal dignity*. We are all created in the same image and likeness of God. So as far as God is concerned, we all have the same basic right to respect and freedom, and we all have the same right to the necessities for sustaining our lives in dignity and freedom: food, clothing, shelter, health care, education, and work.

Though God creates all of us with equal dignity and equal rights, God doesn't create every person equal in terms of advantages such as talents, abilities, intelligence, health, physical strength, and so forth. Take a minute to look around your classroom. God grants everyone equal dignity and rights, but each of you has different talents and limits or needs.

God depends on *us* to share our unique talents, gifts, and qualities with others and to help one another. God intends *us* to be a community—a *co-unity*, a family. In God's eyes, parents and guardians and children have equal dignity and equal rights, but parents and guardians and children aren't equal in other ways. Parents and guardians generally have more experience and education than their young children. They are typically physically stronger. Parents and guardians can earn money that children can't yet

earn. But parents and guardians are supposed to share their experience, strength, and means with their children until the children can take care of themselves. It's much the same with brothers and sisters. Some have special talents or enjoy good health; others may be very young, have disabilities, or suffer poor health. It's taken for granted, though, that siblings share their experiences, talents, and abilities with each other.

God calls the whole human community to be family to each other. Some individuals, groups, or whole countries are blessed with gifts and advantages others don't have. For example, if you were born in a suburb of Pittsburgh, Chicago, or Los Angeles, you started out with a lot more advantages than someone your age who was born in a village in Haiti, a barrio in Rio de Janeiro, or in the inner city of Pittsburgh, Chicago, or Los Angeles.

In God's plan, we all have the responsibility to share our gifts and advantages with our less fortunate brothers and sisters—wherever they were born—because *justice is about taking care of family*. With every right comes responsibility. Morality takes both rights and responsibilities into account.

4

Resource Center

Link to Justice

Ask the students to define *global community*. *(the entire world and all the people who live in it)* Point out that everyone is our neighbor, both people in other countries and those who live nearby. We need to be aware that our pollutants are carried to distant places by wind and water. We need to be aware that our love of certain products may mean that more rain forests will be cleared. We must think about the effects that our actions have on other people.

Link to the Family

Suggest that the students work with family members at home to brainstorm on the following ideas: How can right to truth, to a good name, to personal property, to freedom from physical harm, and so forth, be enjoyed within your family?

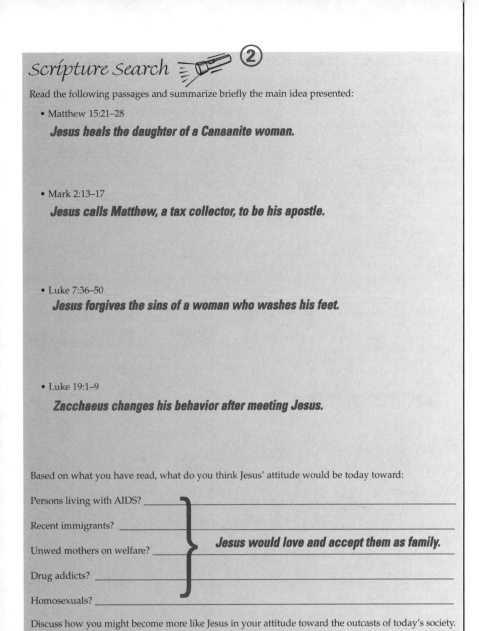

Scripture Search ②

Read the following passages and summarize briefly the main idea presented:

• Matthew 15:21–28

   Jesus heals the daughter of a Canaanite woman.

• Mark 2:13–17

   Jesus calls Matthew, a tax collector, to be his apostle.

• Luke 7:36–50

   Jesus forgives the sins of a woman who washes his feet.

• Luke 19:1–9

   Zacchaeus changes his behavior after meeting Jesus.

Based on what you have read, what do you think Jesus' attitude would be today toward:

Persons living with AIDS? _____

Recent immigrants? _____

Unwed mothers on welfare? _____ } *Jesus would love and accept them as family.*

Drug addicts? _____

Homosexuals? _____

Discuss how you might become more like Jesus in your attitude toward the outcasts of today's society.

5

2. Distribute Bibles. Have students read the passages in the **Scripture Search** activity on page **5**. Allow time for the students to write their answers to the questions. Discuss the students' responses as a class.

The Language of Faith

Explain to the students that how we treat others should not depend on how they treat us. We owe people basic justice, respect, and what is necessary for human life; their God-given humanity demands nothing less. Challenge the students to suggest how this rule could bring change to their daily lives and to the lives of others.

• *Justice* is the cardinal virtue that helps us carry out our moral obligations toward others. Justice is giving each person what he or she is due, not based on material standing or merit, but simply because he or she is a child of God. We work for social justice on earth as a sign of the everlasting justice of God's reign.

• *Injustice* is the opposite of justice—the firm will, which arises from love of God and neighbor, to give each person what he or she is entitled to. The Church teaches that every person has the responsibility to participate in society, and in turn, society must make sure that everyone has the opportunity to do so. Social injustice occurs when people are not allowed to participate fully, as, for example, when they are deprived of the right to shelter, food, a decent education, the right to vote, or the right to speak freely.

Materials

• Bibles

1. Ask for volunteers to take turns reading **The next step** on page **6**. Discuss as needed.

2. Have the students take turns reading aloud the section **Good as gold**. Discuss as needed. Emphasize these points:

   - God, Jesus, and the Church are involved in our living the Golden Rule.

   - God gave us the Ten Commandments.

   - Jesus gave us the Beatitudes.

   - The Church gives us her teachings.

   - All of these help us interpret and live the Golden Rule in our lives.

   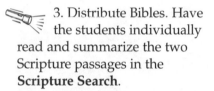 3. Distribute Bibles. Have the students individually read and summarize the two Scripture passages in the **Scripture Search**.

4. When everyone has finished, discuss the two questions in class. Make sure the students realize that the Golden Rule is based on fairness and justice. If I want others to treat me a certain way, then I should be willing to treat them that way, too.

Optional

Have the students work in groups of three to create a modern-day story with the same theme. Call on the groups to share their stories with the class.

Optional

Connect the Golden Rule ("Do unto others what you would want them to do unto you") to our duty to work for social justice. This connection will help the students judge whether they treat others justly.

Materials

- Bibles

The next step 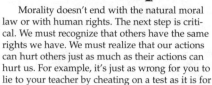 ①

Morality doesn't end with the natural moral law or with human rights. The next step is critical. We must recognize that others have the same rights we have. We must realize that our actions can hurt others just as much as their actions can hurt us. For example, it's just as wrong for you to lie to your teacher by cheating on a test as it is for a friend to lie to you about going to a movie.

That sounds fair enough, but it may take time to sink in. We know when people wrong us because we feel the results of their acts. But we don't always recognize when we've done something wrong to others. We aren't always around to see the results of our actions.

The point is this: Morality is always a two-way street. Any time you have two people, you have two sets of basically identical and equal rights. You have to find a way to live with each other that protects your rights *and* the rights of the other person. Our human dignity requires this.

The more people you put together in a group, the more complicated it gets. In your class, for example, every student (plus the teacher!) has the same right to the truth, to a good name, to personal property, to freedom from physical harm, and so forth. It takes real effort, maturity, and discipline to remember and respect the rights of all other people in your class. This "going beyond" your own self-interest is what we call *moral maturity*.

Good as gold ②

The Bible has another name for moral maturity—the *Golden Rule*. The Golden Rule is basically this: *Do unto others as you would have them do unto you*. Sometimes you'll see the same rule stated in the negative: *Don't do anything to others you would not want to have done to you*.

God has given us the Ten Commandments. Jesus, the Son of God, gave us the law of love and the Beatitudes. All of these revealed directives help us live out the Golden Rule. Church teachings help us interpret these laws for today.

Whether you say it positively or negatively, the Golden Rule works in every culture and in every country. It was true 10,000 years ago. It will be true 10,000 years from now. Regardless of what religion a person follows, this rule is a basic norm for deciding what's right and wrong. To apply the Golden Rule, you simply have to ask yourself two questions:

- How will my action affect others?
- Would I want to be affected that way?

If you can answer both these questions honestly and accurately, you'll know what you should do. Then if you choose not to act that way, you'll also know you are morally wrong.

Scripture Search ③

Read the following Scripture passages and summarize them in your own words.

- Matthew 18:23–35
  A merciless official does not treat his neighbor with the same kindness and understanding with which he has been treated.

- Luke 15:11–32
  Instead of rejecting his wayward son, a father welcomes the son back home and forgives him completely.

Then discuss these questions in class:

1. How does each Scripture passage relate to the Golden Rule? ④

2. What are some practical ways that young people today can follow the Golden Rule?

6

Resource Center

Chapter Overview

This chapter begins by demonstrating that each of us, simply by being human and a child of God, has rights. This inner awareness is the foundation for determining right and wrong; it is the beginning of morality. The next step is crucial, however, and is not always easy. We must come to recognize that other persons have the same rights we have. Before we make a moral decision, we should ask ourselves these two questions: "How will my action affect others?" and "Would I want to be affected that way?" The Golden Rule is a good working norm for determining how we should act in any given situation.

Link to Social Studies

Distribute recent newspapers and magazines. Have the students work in small groups to find one present-day example of a situation that demonstrates observance of the Golden Rule or violations of it.

⑤ Here is one way I can follow the Golden Rule at home this week:

_____

_____

Here is one way I can follow the Golden Rule at school this week:

_____

_____

Knowing vs. doing ⑥

In everyday decisions, normal reasoning based on the natural moral law or the Golden Rule is as terrific a guide as you can find. But morality is more than *knowing* what's right and what's wrong. It also means *doing* what's right and *not doing* what's wrong.

Knowing what we *should* do is usually the easy part of morality. It's much harder to follow through, or act, in ways that are moral.

There are many reasons why people don't do what they know they should do. If we want to grow more morally mature, we need to understand why we don't always follow through on our moral knowledge. Then we need to correct our behavior. Being moral (which is more than knowing about morality) means coming to grips with the gap we all experience between knowing and doing. It means learning how to close that gap when it exists.

God does not leave us alone with this task. First of all, God shares himself with us; this gift is *grace*. And God offers us help and strength—also grace—to make morally mature and good decisions. God helps us bridge the gap between knowing and doing.

7

 5. Explain that **Journal** entries are marked by the notebook and pencil symbol. These are places throughout the book where students may write notes to themselves about their thoughts and feelings. Explain to students that you may periodically collect their journals to check for completion. Allow time now for the students to fill in the two **Journal** entries on page **7**.

6. Ask volunteers to take turns reading aloud **Knowing vs. doing** on page **7**. Discuss as needed.

Optional

We first learn about the common good—what is best for everyone in the community—from our families. With the students, brainstorm specific ways that family members can show respect for one another, provide for one another's needs, and create a peaceful and safe environment in the home.

Optional

Have students read aloud the definition from the dictionary of *golden*. Why is the rule *Do unto others as you would have them do unto you* called "golden"?

Chapter Overview

The chapter recognizes that there is often a gap between knowing how to act and actually acting that way. Dealing with this gap is an ongoing challenge. The more mature we become, the smaller this gap becomes.

Link to Scripture

Have students read aloud *Matthew 7:21–27*. Discuss Jesus' teachings about knowing and doing.

Link to Art

Explain that wisdom is often expressed in short sayings, or proverbs. The gap between *knowing* and *doing* is expressed in phrases such as "Actions speak louder than words" and "Handsome is as handsome does." Have students make posters showing contrasts between knowing and doing, using one of these sayings or one of their own.

Materials

• dictionary (optional)

1. Divide the class into groups of four or five students. Allow time for the students to work with group members to complete the **Being Moral** chart on page **8**. As a class, discuss each group's answers to the chart.

 2. Have a whole-class discussion of the three **Something to talk about** questions. Encourage everyone to participate; accept all reasonable answers.

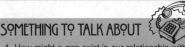

① Being Moral

Work with three or four others to complete the following chart. Then share your answers with the class.

Behavior	Effect on others	Possible reasons for behavior	Ways to correct the behavior
You decide to stay in bed and get up late.	Your parents are late for work. Your brothers and sisters are late for school.		
You cheat on a test.	Students who don't cheat get lower grades.		
You join your friends in teasing or laughing at someone else.	The person feels lonely, hurt, and rejected.		
You refuse to help your brother or sister with household chores.	Your brother or sister misses a favorite TV show.		

② SOMETHING TO TALK ABOUT

1. How might a gap exist in our relationship with God?
2. How might a gap exist in our relationship with nature?
3. How might a gap exist in our relationship with others?

8

Resource Center

The Language of Faith

Morality is the way we put our beliefs into action for what is good. For Christians morality flows from our personal relationship with Christ. We strive to be good because we love and are loved by God, who is all good. This goes beyond keeping the Ten Commandments and obeying the good laws of society. For Catholics morality includes these along with the law of love, the Beatitudes, and the teachings of the Church.

Reason plus faith ③

Morality takes on a whole new meaning if you add faith to natural reason. The basics (such as the natural moral law and the Golden Rule) stay the same, but faith adds a new dimension. For example, Jesus gave the Golden Rule a special twist. He said "You shall love your neighbor as yourself" (Matthew 22:39). This new law of Jesus, received through faith and the power of the Holy Spirit, is lived out in loving action.

Jesus raises morality to the level of love. Love goes beyond what is reasonable and beyond the mathematics of "what is fair." Love includes ideas such as self-sacrifice, forgiving enemies, the common good, and doing the right thing even if others don't treat you the same way. A morality rooted in faith focuses your attention on what is necessary. Faith-based morality stretches you to be the best "you" possible.

Faith, with its added dimension of love, gives a new seriousness to your deliberate choices to ignore what you know is the right thing to do. Faith demands that you view these deliberate choices as more than mistakes. Faith won't let you off the hook with excuses such as "Everybody else is doing it" or "It's no big deal" or "It's nobody's business what I do as long as I don't hurt anyone." Every deliberate choice to do what you know is wrong, no matter how little or how private, takes on a new meaning when you view it with eyes of faith. Faith forces you to deal with the reality of sin and the mystery of evil, consequences of original sin.

Once you bring the faith into the picture, then morality moves into the big leagues. And since you are now old enough to make choices on this level, that's where we want to take this course.

④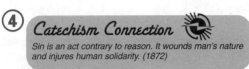

Catechism Connection

Sin is an act contrary to reason. It wounds man's nature and injures human solidarity. (1872)

⑤

Scripture Search ⑥

Read Romans 13:8–14. Discuss what the passage means. Then discuss with the class how love fulfills the law:

- in family situations

_____
_____
_____
_____

- in school situations

_____
_____
_____
_____

- in friendships

_____
_____
_____
_____

9

---

3. Ask volunteers to take turns reading aloud **Reason plus faith** on page **9**.

4. Draw the students' attention to the **Catechism Connection**. Point out that if doing right (morality) is based on reason, then doing wrong (sin) is unreasonable. Sin hurts ourselves and others; it separates us from them.

5. Distribute Bibles. Have the students form small groups to complete the **Scripture Search**.

6. As an entire class, discuss how love fulfills the law.

Optional

Have students create short plays showing the actions of two people: one who follows the law and one who acts in faith, following the higher law of love. Allow time for the students to act out their plays for the class.

Chapter Overview

As the students will learn, morality takes on a whole new meaning when faith is added to natural reason. As Christians, morality flows from our personal relationship with Christ. Jesus raised morality to the level of love when he said, "Love your neighbor in the same way you love yourself." (Matthew 22:39) Students explore what this means throughout the rest of the course.

Link to Scripture

Jesus tells us that even thoughts and emotions, though "private," can be sinful and have consequences. In *Matthew 5:17–26, 38–48*, Jesus commands his followers not only to obey the law, but to go beyond it to the law of love.

The Language of Faith

Righteousness means finding favor with God because of one's innocence or moral uprightness. People who are righteous strive to follow the Ten Commandments and the Beatitudes in their daily lives.

Materials
- Bibles

1. Gather the students, with their books and a pen/pencil, in the designated prayer corner or sacred space. If fire laws permit, light a candle.

2. After the students have become settled, ask a student to read Matthew 22:36–39 (page **10**). Invite the students to reflect silently on what they have heard.

3. After a brief period of silence, ask the students to discuss ways that young people today can live Jesus' law of love. Remind them to show respect for one another by listening and by paying attention to what others are saying. Encourage everyone to say something.

 4. Allow time for the students to complete the **Journal** entry.

5. Pray together the prayer.

Optional

Conclude the **Reflection** by listening to or by singing an appropriate song.

- "Gather Us In" by Marty Haugen from *Gather (Comprehensive)* (GIA), *Glory & Praise* (OCP [NALR]), *Today's Missal* (OCP), *We Celebrate* (J.S. Paluch Co., Inc.).

- "Glory and Praise to Our God" by Dan Schutte from *Glory & Praise* (OCP [NALR]).

- "We Are Called" by David Haas from *Gather (Comprehensive)* (GIA).

- "Whatsoever You Do" by Willard F. Jabusch from *Gather (Comprehensive)* (GIA), *Today's Missal* (OCP), *We Celebrate* (J.S. Paluch Co., Inc.).

10

---

① **Gather for prayer.**  *Reflection*

② *"Teacher, which commandment in the law is the greatest?" [Jesus] said to him, "'You shall love the Lord your God with all your heart, and with all your soul, and with all your mind.' This is the greatest and first commandment. And a second is like it: 'You shall love your neighbor as yourself.'" (Matthew 22:36–39)*

③ Briefly discuss ways that young people today can live the law of love.

 Here is one way I will live the law of love this week: ④
_____
_____

⑤ *Jesus,*
Help me grow each day in love of you and give you thanks for your love of me. Help me grow in maturity and in discipline, so that I may recognize my own rights and the rights of others.
Help me follow the Golden Rule and love my neighbor as I love myself.
Amen.

10

Resource Center

Scripture Background

The Great Commandment: This account appears in slightly different forms in both Matthew's and Luke's Gospels *(Matthew 22:37–39* and *Luke 10:27)*; the version given here is Matthew's. The Great Commandment was stated in *Deuteronomy 6:4* and *Leviticus 19:18* and was an honored part of Jewish teaching.

Catechism Background

For background on the Great Commandment, see the *Catechism of the Catholic Church* (#2055).

Reference Sources

For help in addressing the students' questions about the unit's topics, see:

- *Kids 'n Values: A Handbook for Helping Kids Discover Christian Values* by John A. Flanagan (Liguori Publications, 1995).
- *Catholic Source Book* edited by Rev. Peter Klein (BROWN-ROA, 1990).

HOMEWORK ⑥

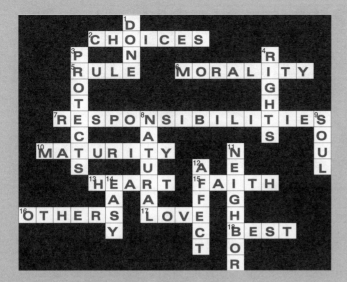

1. People everywhere have certain (4 down).
2. (6 across) begins with our ability to name certain acts as wrong.
3. You must live the way that (3 down) your rights and the rights of others.
4. To respect the rights of (16 across) takes effort, maturity, and discipline.
5. It is the "going beyond" one's own rights that we call moral (10 across).
6. Don't do anything to others you would not want to have (1 down) to you.
7. Moral responsibility begins with applying the Golden (5 across).
8. It is important to ask how my action will (12 down) others.
9. Knowing what we should do is the (14 down) part.
10. If you move beyond natural reason to (15 across), morality takes on a whole new meaning.
11. You shall love your (11 down) as yourself.
12. Jesus raises morality to the level of (17 across).
13. Faith-based morality stretches you to be the (18 across) possible you.
14. Faith gives a new seriousness to your deliberate (2 across).
15. The (8 down) law has its roots in God's plan for things.
16. You shall love the Lord your God with all your (13 across), and with all your (9 down), and with all your mind.
17. Morality takes both rights and (7 across) into account.

11

Answers to the Homework

1. rights
2. Morality
3. protects
4. others
5. maturity
6. done
7. Rule
8. affect
9. easy
10. faith
11. neighbor
12. love
13. best
14. choices
15. natural
16. heart; soul
17. responsibilities

 6. Remind the students to do the **Homework** and to review the chapter for the next class.

Optional

There will be a short quiz at the beginning of the next class.

Multimedia Resources

Jazz Band Blues, produced by Twenty-Third Publications (video) (BROWN-ROA, 1-800-922-7696).

Love, the Main Ingredient, produced by the Archdiocese of St. Paul-Minneapolis (video) (BROWN-ROA, 1-800-922-7696).

Math Class Mischief, produced by Twenty-Third Publications (video) (BROWN-ROA, 1-800-922-7696).

Rock Ticket Trouble, produced by Twenty-Third Publications (video) (BROWN-ROA, 1-800-922-7696).

Stories of the Human Spirit, "The Father's Bowl," produced by ACTA Publications (video) (BROWN-ROA, 1-800-922-7696).

Street Hockey Hassle, produced by Twenty-Third Publications (video) (BROWN-ROA, 1-800-922-7696).

Swim Team Splash, produced by Twenty-Third Publications (video) (BROWN-ROA, 1-800-922-7696)

Name: _____ Date: _____

1: What's Right? What's Wrong?
Review Quiz

True or False

____ 1. Morality flows from our personal relationship with Christ.

____ 2. All are created equal in dignity, rights, and advantages such as talents and abilities.

____ 3. We don't always recognize when we've done something wrong to others.

____ 4. The Golden Rule states that you may treat others the way they treat you.

____ 5. Being moral means coming to grips with the gap we experience between knowing and doing.

____ 6. Love is based on what is reasonable and fair.

Fill in the Blanks

1. The _____ norms of morality are based on the natural moral law.

2. Each of us, simply by being a child of God, has _____.

3. God calls the whole human community to be _____ to each other.

4. "Going beyond" your own self interest is what we call _____ _____.

5. God shares himself with us; this gift is _____.

6. Morality takes on a whole new meaning if you add _____ to natural reason.

BROWN-ROA, a division of Harcourt Brace & Company

1: What's Right? What's Wrong?
Review Quiz

Essay

1. Explain how the way in which God sees justice influences relationships between members of families, of communities, and of nations.

2. Explain the meaning of and give examples of the statement "Morality is a two-way street."

3. Explain ways in which adding faith to reason could change completely a person's life and help change the whole world.

2

Lesson Procedure

Academic Goal: To understand the nature of conscience—how it develops and its crucial role in guiding moral behavior.

Attitudinal Goal: To appreciate the many influences that affect conscience development and to take responsibility for developing and defining our conscience.

1. Go over the chapter 1 **Homework** answers, found on page **11**.

2. Review chapter 1 by giving the students a quiz. Reproduce page **11A** and/or page **11B** and give one to each student. After the students have completed the quiz, collect them to correct later. If you wish, correct the quizzes in class with the students.

Optional

As the students take the review quiz, collect their textbooks and journals. Scan the pages to make sure the students are completing the **Journal** activities. Also scan for indications of problems that should be addressed.

3. Have the students take turns reading aloud **The ability to judge** on page **12**.

4. With the help of the students, define *conscience*. This may be a less than precise exercise. It is more important to have the students articulate their understanding of conscience than it is to instill them with theological exactness. Life is a process and, generally, students will have plenty of time to refine their definitions as they mature.

---

① **Discuss** homework assignment. ② **Give** students the review quiz.

2 Our Conscience and Convictions

③ **The ability to judge** ④ *Define* conscience.
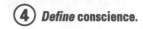

In the last chapter, you discovered that morality involves two things. First of all, morality means **knowing** what's right and what's wrong. And second, morality means **doing** what we know is right.

In this chapter, we're going to focus more on your ability to judge what is good or bad in a particular situation. We call this ability *conscience*.

Conscience is part of the human ability to think and to reason. Conscience helps you make judgments about what's right and what's wrong. To a large extent, your conscience measures what's good and what's bad by certain God-given standards, or norms. Many of these have been mentioned before: the Ten Commandments, the Golden Rule, the law of love, and the Beatitudes.

These norms help protect human rights. For example, the norm "murder is wrong" protects the right to life. The norm "stealing is wrong" protects people's right to have personal property. The norm "lying is wrong" protects everyone's right to know the truth.

Because all human beings have the same rights, it would seem that all people should have the same ideas about what's good or bad. We should all have the same kind of conscience. But we don't. Why? Read the two cases on the next page to see if you can figure out the answer.

12

Chapter 1 Quiz Answers

True or False

1. T	4. F
2. F	5. T
3. T	6. F

Fill in the Blanks

1. objective	4. moral maturity
2. rights	5. grace
3. family	6. faith

Essay

1. God sees justice as taking care of family, which includes the community of our family, our local community, and the human community. God grants everyone equal dignity and rights, but each person has different talents and limits or needs. God depends on us to share our unique talents, gifts, and qualities with others and to help one another.

⑤ ¿ ¿ ¿What would you do? ? ? ?

Case 1

Karen is walking around the supermarket finding the items on her father's shopping list. When she passes the candy shelves, she takes one of her favorite candy bars. She eats it while she shops and throws the wrapper behind the cereal boxes. When she pays for her groceries, she doesn't mention the candy bar she ate.

This is Karen's reasoning: *I don't steal because I think it's wrong to steal. Eating the candy bar isn't stealing. My dad said that big supermarket chains expect that kind of thing. They already overcharge us for it, so we may as well take advantage when we can.*

Was Karen's decision moral? _____

Why? _____
_____
_____
_____
_____

Case 2

José is walking around the supermarket finding the items on his family's shopping list. When he passes the candy shelves, he takes one of his favorite candy bars. He eats it while he shops. When he is at the checkout counter, he produces the candy wrapper and tells the clerk to include it in the cost of the groceries.

This is José's thinking: *I ate the candy bar, but I paid for it later. My grandfather used to manage a supermarket. He told me how much money the stores lose each month because of that kind of thing. It runs into the thousands of dollars! Everybody ends up paying higher prices because some people take a twenty-five cent item here and a fifty-cent item there.*

Was José's decision moral? _____

Why? _____
_____
_____
_____

If you were faced with the choice, what reasons would you have for your decision?
_____
_____
_____
_____
_____
_____
_____

⑥ Discussion of activity.

13

5. Have the students work individually on the **What would you do?** activity.

6. Discuss the students' answers to the activity. Accept all answers. Do not express any judgment of your own at this time.

Optional

Have the students write a one-page letter to Karen or José explaining why they think Karen or José's decision was moral. Invite them to look to their answers for the last two questions in the **What would you do?** activity as a basis for their letter. Encourage the students to provide examples from Jesus' life and the life of others, or to cite the Ten Commandments, the Beatitudes, the law of love, or the teachings of the Church to support their position.

Optional

On a table in your classroom, display small objects that can be taken and easily hidden. Have students write a fictional court case describing a situation similar to the two stories on page **13**. In their story, one of the objects on the table is taken and two people who have taken it give different reasons for their actions.

2. Any time you have two people, you have two sets of basically identical and equal rights. You have to find a way to live with each other that protects your rights *and* the rights of the other person. Our human dignity requires this. This is the meaning of the phrase "Morality is a two-way street."

3. Answers may vary. Jesus raises morality to the level of love. Love goes beyond what is reasonable and beyond the mathematics of "what is fair." Love includes ideas such as self-sacrifice, forgiving enemies, the common good, and doing the right thing even if others don't treat you the same way. A morality rooted in faith focuses your attention on what is necessary. It stretches you to be the best "you" possible.

Materials

• small objects (optional)

1. Have the students take turns reading aloud the text on page **14**. Discuss as needed. Make sure the students understand the concept of "personalized" conscience, that each person has slightly different ways of viewing what's right and what's wrong.

2. Ask another volunteer to read aloud the **F.Y.I.** section or allow time for the students to read this section silently on their own. Discuss whether or not the students agree with the statement.

Personalized conscience

Both Karen and José agree with the norm "stealing is wrong." So far, so good. But they have different views on what stealing actually is. They have "personalized" the general concept of stealing in different ways. Karen is convinced she's right when she eats the candy bar and doesn't pay for it. She doesn't see it as stealing, and so she doesn't feel guilty.

Most people would agree that there is a defect in Karen's reasoning. After all, if everyone reasoned the way Karen does, it wouldn't be long before most stores would go out of business or they'd have to charge such high prices that only the rich could afford to eat. Karen's act was wrong even if she wasn't aware of her guilt. What she did was, in fact, stealing.

How did Karen and José develop such different concepts of stealing? Some of it had to do with their family's influence. José's grandfather taught him one way of thinking; Karen's father taught her another. The same is true for most of the people in the world. We end up with a more or less unique conscience because we have different experiences and influences that shape our conscience.

However, we have a responsibility to educate and form our conscience. This task is a lifelong process. While the people in our lives can influence us in the wrong direction as well as the right, we can rely on God's Spirit at work in the teachings of the Church to guide us in the right direction.

 ② **F.Y.I.**

According to an old saying, "People are as good as their teachers."

14

Resource Center

The Language of Faith

Conscience comes from a Latin word meaning "knowledge within." Our conscience gives us the inner knowledge to judge a situation and then act in a way that shows love and respect for ourselves and others. *Conscience* is free will and reason working together to distinguish right from wrong. Many people have described this faculty as an "inner voice." A well-formed conscience helps us adhere to moral standards even if they conflict with our own desires and wants. The Church teaches that in all moral situations, we are obliged to follow our well-formed conscience. We have an obligation to educate and inform our conscience.

③ How about you?

Although God has provided you with all the help you need to make good decisions, many other things influence you and affect your conscience, your ability to judge what is good or bad. Take some time to think about the following influences and how they have shaped your concept of what's right and what's wrong. Write down your thoughts in the space below.

Influence	What's Right? What's Wrong?
My family (especially my parents)	
My friends	
My neighborhood or town	
My country	
My school	
TV	
Books or magazines	
Movies or videos	
Music	

④ Class discussion.

When it comes to stealing, here's what I think is right and wrong:

_____

_____

_____

I think this way because:

_____

_____

_____

_____

15

3. Allow time for the students to work individually to complete the **How about you?** chart.

4. As a class, discuss the chart. Ask volunteers to share their insights.

5. Allow time for the students to complete the two **Journal** entries.

Chapter Overview

The chapter begins with several stories illustrating how good people can approach the same problem in entirely different ways. In that context, the idea of conscience is introduced and explained as having two components: an ability to judge and a set of norms used for judging. We all start out with the same general norms (for example, lying is wrong, stealing is wrong, murder is wrong, and so forth). But family, culture, and other influences shape, or "personalize," these norms. Hence, two people can arrive at different ideas of what is right and wrong when looking at the same problem.

Assessment Tip

Invite the students to answer these questions as a way to help them check their actions: Do I ever tell myself it's okay to do something because other people are doing it? Or because no one will ever notice or find out? Or because no one really gets hurt?

1. Call on volunteers to read aloud the two cases on page **16**. Ask the students for their reactions to the cases. Which person, Julie or Parnda, comes closest to their own view and attitude? Why?

2. Have students take turns reading aloud the text.

 3. As an entire class, discuss the two **Something to talk about** questions.

 4. Allow time for the students to work on their **Journal** entry.

Developing your conscience

Consider the following cases:

Case 1
Julie lives in a small town in the Midwest. On her way home from cheerleader practice, she sees an old man lying on the sidewalk. No one else is around. She immediately runs over to see if he's hurt. She feels it's her Christian duty to help any way she can.

Case 2
Parnda lives in Calcutta, India. He's coming home from school. There's an ill woman lying on the sidewalk. He carefully steps around her. He'd like to help, but he feels it would be a waste of time even to try. After all, he'll pass at least ten such people before he reaches home. There's not much one person can do to help.

Both Julie and Parnda agree that it's good to help people in need. But they have different convictions about their responsibility for helping. Julie is convinced she can do something to help, so that's the way she acts. Parnda is convinced there isn't much he can do to help everybody, so that's the way he acts.

Although Parnda has a point, doing something to help the ill woman would be better than doing nothing at all. Even if he can't help everybody, he could help somebody. If everyone held Parnda's convictions, then none of us would ever try to help others. It seems that Parnda needs to develop his conscience a bit further.

The same is true for everyone. As we mature, we need to keep developing and refining our conscience. This job is not easy. We have to keep checking out what has been influencing us to think the way we do. We have to look at our convictions in an objective, honest way.

It's very difficult to become "unconvinced" once you've become sure about something. After all, you're *sure* you're right.

SOMETHING TO TALK ABOUT

1. What do you think it would take to convince Karen (page 13) that what she did is actually stealing?

2. What do you think it would take to convince Parnda that maybe he should try to do something to help?

What would it take to get you to change some of your present convictions?

_____
_____
_____
_____
_____

16

Resource Center

Link to Justice

Bring to class magazine or newspaper articles about Mother Teresa. Allow students to read the various articles. Discuss how Mother Teresa might have acted in the situation described on page 16. What would have been her feelings toward the man or woman lying on the sidewalk?

Link to Faith Community

The Catholic Church has established its own schools and religious education programs under the guidance of bishops and other authorities. How are the Church's educational activities involved in conscience formation?

Catechism Background

For more information on conscience and the responsibility to make sure our conscience is well formed, you may want to read the *Catechism of the Catholic Church* (#s 1776–1802).

Let's get practical

(5) You have a conscience—the ability to judge what's right and what's wrong according to certain norms. Your norms are your personal *convictions*. You've been developing these convictions gradually, sometimes without being aware of it. The world in which you have been growing up (family, friends, neighborhood, TV, etc.) has played a big role in shaping your personal convictions.

(7) Most of your convictions are probably already pretty much in line with the norms God uses to judge right from wrong, such as the Ten Commandments. But there's also a good chance that some of your convictions have defects in them. They aren't in line with God's norms. The challenge is to keep developing and refining your "personalized" conscience. This means, among other things, discovering and then changing your defective convictions.

How can you do this? Here are four suggestions:

1. **Be very honest with yourself.** If you're really honest, you can usually discover your defective convictions. Many defective convictions are an "excuse" for taking the easy way out of a tough situation. Cheating on tests is a good example. Some people are sincerely convinced that cheating is not lying. Obviously cheating for a few minutes is easier than studying for several hours, especially if you get an A by cheating and only a C after studying for a couple of hours. Being "convinced" that cheating isn't wrong gives people a nice excuse to avoid the hard work of studying.

2. **Be guided by God's word and the teachings of the Church.** In the Bible, we read the story of God's covenant with the Jewish people and its extension to all people in Jesus. Both the old and the new covenants spell out laws for right living. Over the centuries as times have changed, the Church has interpreted and applied these laws for each generation. These teachings reach you through the readings and homilies at Mass and your religion class. They become more a part of your decision making as you read the Bible and pray over your decisions.

(6) Class discussion.

3. **Accept advice from others, especially more experienced people such as your teachers and parents.** Sure, parents and teachers aren't automatically right all the time. They can be victims of mistaken ideas and can have defective convictions of their own. But, as a general rule, when older people who love you very much challenge a conviction you have, it's usually time to reevaluate what you think.

4. **Look carefully at messages you get from popular culture (TV, songs, movie stars, video games, etc.).** Popular culture usually produces convictions that are the result of shallow thinking, such as "everybody does it" or "it's okay if nobody gets hurt" or "go for the gusto." Don't take this the wrong way. We're not saying that everything on TV or in popular music is bad. But you should be cautious. Don't settle for shallow thinking or "quick fix" solutions to the moral issues in life. What you see in the media is not a good guide for making moral decisions.

To sum up, then, there are four practical steps you can take to continue developing your "personalized" conscience: Be honest, be guided by truth, be open, and be critical.

F.Y.I. ✎ (8)

By the time you finish eighth grade, you will have spent 7,200 hours in school, but you will have watched 8,000 hours of television!

(9) Catechism Connection

. . . A well-formed conscience is upright and truthful. It forms its judgments according to reason, in conformity with the true good willed by the Creator. . . . (1783)

The education of the conscience is a lifelong task. . . . (1784)

5. Call on a student to read aloud the first paragraph of **Let's get practical**.

6. Discuss the text by asking the students these questions:

   - What are some common convictions people your age hold?

   - Are all of these convictions true?

   - What is an example of a conviction you would never change?

7. Ask volunteers to read aloud the remaining text on page **17**.

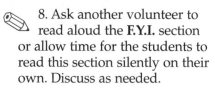 8. Ask another volunteer to read aloud the **F.Y.I.** section or allow time for the students to read this section silently on their own. Discuss as needed.

9. Draw the students' attention to the **Catechism Connection**. Ask the students why they think that education of the conscience is a lifelong task. Make sure they realize that all people, regardless of age, are learning new things about the meaning of what's right and what's wrong.

Optional

Discuss with the students some of the techniques of persuasion that advertisers use in order to influence people's desires, feelings, and behaviors. In the discussion, include testimonials (experts' endorsements of an idea or a product), the bandwagon technique (a "join the crowd" appeal), and glittering generalities (sweeping, unsubstantiated statements). Show newspaper and magazine advertisements that use these techniques. Then challenge the students to find and share other examples.

Chapter Overview

As the students will learn, our personalized conscience may have defects in it. Refining our personalized conscience requires that we do four things:

- be honest with ourselves;
- be guided by God's word and the teachings of the Church;
- be open to the advice of more experienced people; and
- be critical of popular norms found in our culture.

Link to Reading

Bring to class some reviews of contemporary TV shows and movies that have appeared in Catholic publications. How might reading these help form one's conscience about popular culture?

1. Have the students take turns reading aloud **Judging guilt and innocence** on page **18**.

 2. Distribute Bibles. Have the students work alone to read and summarize Matthew 7:1–5.

3. Hold a class discussion of the two questions on page **18**. Encourage everyone to participate. If needed, remind the students to listen to one another and to respect one another's answers.

---

① Judging guilt and innocence

Ignorance of the law is no excuse for breaking the law. For example, suppose you are older and are driving a car. If you miss the sign and start driving the wrong way down a one-way street, you'll probably get a ticket. You're guilty of breaking the law in the legal, or *objective*, sense. Personally, on the *subjective* level, you're innocent because you honestly didn't mean to break the law. But you still have to pay the fine.

The difference between legal (objective) guilt and personal (subjective) guilt is very important. Society has to judge us objectively, on our actions. But only God can judge us subjectively, on our thoughts and motives. For example, think about a poor woman who is desperate. She steals food from a store to feed her starving children. If she's caught, she'll likely be punished because she broke the law. But what she did may not be considered wrong in God's eyes.

What does that mean for us? It means that we, like society, can recognize when laws are broken. We can say that people who break these laws are *objectively* guilty. But we have no right to judge people at the *subjective*, personal level. That's God's job.

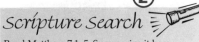

Read Matthew 7:1–5. Summarize it here:
Don't judge others for you, too, will be judged.
_____
_____
_____
_____

Then discuss these questions in class: ③

1. How does this Scripture passage relate to students today?

2. Do you think we can ever judge someone's subjective guilt? Why or why not?

18

Materials

• Bible

Resource Center

Chapter Overview

The chapter examines what is involved in each of these tasks and distinguishes between objective and subjective guilt or innocence. As the students will learn, a person may be objectively guilty of breaking a law and therefore be accountable objectively. But subjectively, he or she may remain innocent in God's eyes.

Catechism Background

For more information on judging the morality of human acts, read the *Catechism of the Catholic Church* (#s 1749–56).

How God judges

As Christians, we believe that God always judges us according to what our properly-formed conscience *sincerely* judges to be right or wrong. For example, God won't judge Karen as a thief or Parnda as selfish because they sincerely thought they did the right thing. That's how God judges you, too. But don't use this as an excuse. You have a conscience that you have to keep developing and refining.

When you were younger, you weren't able to evaluate your convictions. All you knew about right and wrong was what you learned from your family in your own "little" world. But as you get older, you can now evaluate and affirm or rethink what you learned as a child. This means bringing your conscience in line with how God sees things and with the norms God uses to judge good and bad.

As we said earlier, developing and refining your conscience is a lifelong process. You'll always need to keep stretching in order to be honest, to be guided by the truth, to be open, and to be critical. You'll always need to keep trying to bring your convictions in line with God's norms about right and wrong. As you grow up, this will require an adult faith, which is the topic of the next chapter.

  # Heroes and heroines

Every culture has certain heroes and heroines it holds up as moral models for its children. To discover this influence on your conscience, answer the following questions. Discuss your answers in small groups.

1. Who were your heroes and heroines when you were little?

2. What did these heroes or heroines teach you about right and wrong?

3. Who are your heroes and heroines now?

4. What are they teaching you about right and wrong?

Form groups and discuss.

If time permits, work with your group to describe the ideal hero or heroine for today's young people. Record your notes here. Then share this description with the class.

 THE IDEAL HERO OR HEROINE

 Class sharing.

19

4. Have students take turns reading aloud the text. Discuss as needed. Make sure the students realize that God always judges us with love and understanding. God not only sees our behavior; God also sees our reasons and motives behind our behavior.

5. Allow time for the students to work individually to complete the four questions in the **Heroes and heroines** activity on page **19**.

6. Have the students form groups of three or four to discuss their answers to the four questions.

7. Allow three or four minutes for group members to work together to come up with a description of the ideal hero or heroine.

8. At the end of the allotted work time, call on each group to share its description with the class.

Chapter Overview

The goal of conscience formation means continually refining and challenging our "personalized" conscience so that it reflects the mind of Christ—that we begin to see right and wrong as God does.

Link to Reading

Read aloud in class the story of Zacchaeus the tax collector in *Luke 19:1–10*. How did Zacchaeus bring his conscience "in line" with how God sees things? Why was Zacchaeus described as "a sinner"? What good resolutions did he make after seeing Jesus?

1. Gather the students, with their books and a pen/pencil, in the designated prayer corner or sacred space. If fire laws permit, light a candle.

2. After the students have become settled, ask a student to read Sirach 14:2 (page **22**). Invite the students to reflect silently on what they have heard.

3. After a brief period of silence, ask the students to discuss ways that young people today can be honest, open, and critical when dealing with moral convictions. Remind the students to show respect for one another by listening and by paying attention to what others are saying. Encourage everyone to say something.

 4. Allow time for the students to complete the **Journal** entries.

5. Pray together the prayer.

Optional

Conclude the **Reflection** by listening to or by singing an appropriate song.

- "Anthem" by Tom Conry from *Glory & Praise* (OCP [NALR]), *Today's Missal* (OCP), *Gather (Comprehensive)* (GIA).

- "Speak, Lord," by Gary Ault from *Glory & Praise* (OCP [NALR]).

- "We Are Many Parts" by Marty Haugen from *Gather (Comprehensive)* (GIA), *We Celebrate* (J.S. Paluch Co., Inc.), *Today's Missal* (OCP).

- "You Are Near" by Dan Schutte from *Gather (Comprehensive)* (GIA), *Today's Missal* (OCP), *Glory & Praise* (OCP [NALR]).

---

① **Gather for prayer.**

② *Reflection*

Happy are those whose hearts do not condemn them, and who have not given up their hope.
(Sirach 14:2)

Briefly discuss ways that young people today can be honest, guided by truth, open, and critical when dealing with moral convictions. ③ ④

Here is one way I will be honest this week with myself:
_____
_____

Here is one way I will be guided this week by the truth:
_____
_____

Here is one way I will be open this week to the advice of parents and teachers:
_____
_____

Here is one way I will be critical this week of the convictions I find in popular culture:
_____
_____

⑤ *Jesus,*
Help me develop the ability to make good judgments.
Help me identify any defective convictions I may have, and give me the strength to correct them.
Help me get my personal conscience in line with your norms.
Amen.

20

Resource Center

Reference Sources

For help in addressing the students' questions about the unit's topics, see:

- *Conscience in Conflict—How to Make Moral Choices* by Kenneth R. Overberg SJ (St. Anthony Messenger Press, 1991).

- *Whatever Happened to Sin?—The Truth about Catholic Morality* by Charles E. Bouchard OP (Liguori Publications, 1996).

HOMEWORK   ⑥

Before the next class, watch one of the following programs:

• a video,

• a Saturday morning cartoon,

• an MTV show,

• a soap opera, or

• a sitcom

Evaluate the program by answering these questions.

1. What was the name of the program and what was it about?

2. What message did the program present about what's right and what's wrong?

3. Do you agree or disagree with the message? Why?

4. What do you think Jesus would say about the program's message? Why?

Be prepared to discuss your answers at the next class meeting.

21

 6. Remind the students to do the **Homework** and to review the chapter for the next class.

Optional

There will be a short quiz at the beginning of the next class.

Multimedia Resources

A Case of Conscience: Dealing with Peer Pressure, produced by Robert Blaskey (video) (BROWN-ROA, 1-800-922-7696).

The Power and Impact of the Media, produced by American Portrait Films International (video) (BROWN-ROA, 1-800-922-7696).

Exploring Media with Today's Parables, produced by Robert Blaskey (video) (BROWN-ROA, 1-800-922-7696).

Heroes of Faith, produced by Heart of the Nation (video) (BROWN-ROA, 1-800-922-7696).

Stories of the Human Spirit, "The Irritable Man," produced by ACTA Publications (video) (BROWN-ROA, 1-800-922-7696).

Name: _____ Date: _____

2: Our Conscience and Convictions
Review Quiz

True or False

____ 1. Morality only involves the ability to know right from wrong.

____ 2. Everyone shares the exact same ideas about what is right and wrong.

____ 3. As you mature, you have to keep developing and refining your conscience.

____ 4. Some people really believe their defective convictions; other people use such convictions as an excuse for taking the easy way out of a tough situation.

____ 5. Being open to advice plays a big role in the development of a mature conscience.

____ 6. Society judges guilt or innocence at the objective level.

Fill in the Blanks

1. The standards by which people judge what is right and what is wrong are called

_____.

2. Your family, friends, neighborhood, and school help shape your _____

_____, your idea of right and wrong.

3. _____ is the ability to judge what is right and wrong.

4. As we mature, we need to keep _____ and _____ our personalized conscience.

5. Practical steps to developing a mature conscience are to be honest, to be guided by _____

_____ and the _____ of the _____, to be open, and to be

_____.

6. Only God can judge us _____.

BROWN-ROA, a division of Harcourt Brace & Company

2: Our Conscience and Convictions
Review Quiz

Essay

1. What are God's standards or norms for measuring what's good and what's wrong?

2. Explain the four suggestions for changing your defective convictions.

3. Explain the difference between objective and subjective guilt and why this difference is important.

3
Lesson Procedure

Academic Goal: To understand that having a morality based on faith means putting on the mind and heart of Jesus.

Attitudinal Goal: To work at becoming truly aware of the suffering of our brothers and sisters and to allow God's word to guide our thinking and God's Spirit to guide our actions.

1. Go over the chapter 2 **Homework** questions, found on page **21**. Encourage everyone to share something.

2. Review chapter 2 by giving the students a quiz. Reproduce page **21A** and/or page **21B** and give one to each student. After the students have completed the quiz, collect them to correct later. If you wish, correct the quizzes in class with the students.

Optional

As the students take the review quiz, collect their textbooks and journals. Scan the pages to make sure the students are completing the **Journal** activities. Also scan for indications of problems that should be addressed.

3. Have the students take turns reading aloud the text on page **22**. Discuss the text by asking these questions:

- What are some aids people use in order to see better? *(eyeglasses, magnifying glasses, slanted mirrors for looking around corners, microscopes, telescopes, and so forth)*

- How does faith help people see better? *(It helps us see the "bigger picture.")*

---

① *Discuss homework assignment.* **②** *Give students the review quiz.*

3 The Bottom Line

A different slant ③

In the last chapter, we saw how family, culture, and education can give people a slightly different slant on how they view basic moral norms. Faith gives us a different slant on morality, too. It gives us a new way to see and to interpret the moral norms that we already know through reason.

Perhaps it can be explained like this: Every month on clear nights, you can look up and see the moon. It's familiar. It's there. Then suppose a friend invites you to view the moon through the telescope she got for her birthday. When you look through the telescope, it's like seeing the moon for the first time. It has a whole new look because you can see more detail.

It's much the same way when you look at yourself and your world through the eyes of faith. Faith is like a powerful telescope. It helps you to see the "bigger picture."

By this time in your life, you're probably getting to know yourself fairly well. You know a lot more about human nature—and about right and wrong—than you did three or four years ago. Much of life may seem rather familiar now. But if you look at life through the eyes of faith (that is, through the eyes of Jesus), it's a whole new view.

When you see things through the eyes of faith, the reverse can happen too. What might at first seem like a routine act could take on a very heroic, even saintly, meaning. For example, if you decide not to buy a candy bar so you can buy something else for yourself, big deal. But suppose you save the money so that you can give it to a missionary or to a collection that helps people who are hungry. Your faith tells you that those nameless hungry people are God's children too. You have a moral responsibility to treat them as your own brothers and sisters. Now your decision not to buy a candy bar takes on a whole new meaning.

Having a morality that is based on faith means putting on the mind and heart of Jesus. It means thinking and acting like he thought and acted. It means treating others in the same way that Jesus would have treated them.

22

Chapter 2 Quiz Answers

True or False

1. F	4. T
2. F	5. T
3. T	6. T

Fill in the Blanks

1. norms
2. personalized conscience
3. conscience
4. developing, refining (any order)
5. God's word; teaching; church; critical
6. subjectively

Essay

1. Some of God's standards, or norms, that he uses to judge what's good and what's bad include the Ten Commandments, the Golden Rule, the law of love, and the Beatitudes.

The mind and heart of Jesus ④ ⑤

Imagine yourself in each of the following situations.

Your friend lost her wallet and now has no money for lunch.

The new student doesn't seem very happy, but you've already made plans with your friends.

Your mother wants to borrow your favorite sweatshirt. You're planning on wearing it tomorrow.

Your friends' older brother has AIDS and is sick in the hospital.

Your cousin stole a car and now is in juvenile hall.

The St. Vincent de Paul Society is collecting money for poor families.

Decide what would be a reasonable response.

Read Matthew 26:31–46. Decide how Jesus might respond to each situation.

After you have finished writing your answers, discuss them in a group with three or four others.

 ⑥

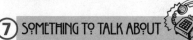 ⑦ SOMETHING TO TALK ABOUT

As a group, share your answers about Jesus with the class. Why do you think Jesus would act this way?

23

---

4. Have the students work alone to complete the first part of **The mind and heart of Jesus** activity on page **23**.

5. Distribute Bibles. Have the students continue working alone to complete the second part of the activity.

6. When everyone has finished filling in the chart, have the students form groups of four or five to discuss the chart answers.

 7. Hold a class discussion of the **Something to talk about** question. Encourage everyone to say something.

Optional

Have the students read Matthew 9:9–13. Many times Jesus was criticized for associating with "sinners" and those considered "unclean." Ask the students: What reasons does Jesus give for his actions? What reasons might you give if friends criticize you for acting as Jesus did?

---

2. The four suggestions for changing defective convictions include: 1) be very honest with yourself; 2) be guided by God's word and the teachings of the Church; 3) accept advice from others, especially more experienced people; 4) look carefully at messages you get from popular culture.

3. Objective guilt is when you break the law in the legal sense. Subjective guilt is whether or not you meant to break the law, your personal feelings about what you did and why you did it. The difference is important because society has to judge us objectively, on our actions, but only God can judge us subjectively, on our thoughts and motives.

Materials

- Bibles

1. Ask volunteers to take turns reading aloud **Compassion means "to suffer with"** on page **24**. Discuss as needed.

2. Divide the students into small groups. Allow time for the groups to develop T-shirt or bumper sticker slogans for the **Think Positive** activity. Instruct the groups to print their slogans on poster board and decorate the poster using markers. Display the slogans in the classroom.

Optional

Distribute recent newspapers and news magazines. Have the students work in groups of three to find five news stories that deserve our compassion and five news stories that are not all that important. When the groups have finished working, call on them to give examples. Make sure the students realize that we must first notice the suffering of others before we can be motivated to relieve that suffering.

Materials
- poster board
- markers
- newspapers (optional)
- news magazines (optional)

---

① Compassion means "to suffer with"

There are many places in the Gospels where it says "Jesus looked with pity" or "Jesus was deeply moved" or "Jesus felt compassion for . . ." In one place, it even says Jesus openly wept at the thought of the suffering his Jewish brothers and sisters were going to have to experience. Jesus didn't just passively observe the pain of others, however. Jesus felt their pain and entered into it. It touched him so deeply he felt moved to act.

This same compassion is the key for us. Entering into the suffering of others gives a greater sense of urgency to eliminating injustice. The closer you are to the pain of others, the more you will want to ease that pain. Compassion is a very natural emotion for us. The real trick is first noticing, then being genuinely sensitive to the suffering of others.

Not enough time is given to creating awareness that allows us to enter into the suffering of our brothers and sisters elsewhere. We have to work at becoming truly aware of the suffering of our brothers and sisters—both in our hometown and throughout the world. Jesus used the image of the reign of God to describe how we should live together as a family. Jesus taught that God reigns when we allow God's word to guide our thinking and God's Spirit to guide our actions. When we allow God to "rule" over our minds and hearts, the result is a just society—a true family, the family God intends us to be.

② Think Positive

Many T-shirt slogans encourage violence, vengeance, and prejudice. Can you think of any that promote compassion? In your group, try to develop a compassionate slogan for a T-shirt or a bumper sticker. Write your slogan here:

_____

_____

24

Resource Center
The Language of Faith

- *Compassion* means "to suffer with" another, to feel that person's suffering and to desire to lessen his or her pain. The Gospels tell us that Jesus frequently felt and showed compassion for others. For example, Jesus fed the hungry crowd *(Matthew 14:13–21)*, cured lepers *(Mark 1:40–45)*, spent time with sinners *(Matthew 9:9–13)*, and consoled those who were grieving *(Luke 7:11–17)*.

- *Reign* is another word for kingdom or power. God's reign is a kingdom of justice, love, and peace, announced by Jesus Christ, present in our midst, and yet to come in fullness.

- *Faith* is our response to God's invitation to enter a personal, trusting relationship with him. If we have *faith*, we trust in God's promises and accept his invitation by the way we live our lives.

Scripture Search  ③

Read Mark 8:1–9 and write a short summary of what this passage means.

__Jesus feeds four thousand people with seven loaves of bread and a few fish.__

___

___

Based on local, national, or international injustices, list three groups of people for whom you feel sad. Then try to name one practical thing this compassion moves you to do to help these groups.

1. _____
2. _____
3. _____

Compose a short prayer asking Jesus to help you develop the same kind of compassion he had.

___

___

___

___

More about Jesus ④

The most obvious place to discover the mind and heart of Jesus is in the New Testament of the Bible. But this is not as easy as it sounds. Consider these examples:

- One time in the Gospels, Jesus tells his disciples they must obey the scribes and Pharisees because they are the legal leaders. Another time, Jesus warns his disciples to beware of the teachings of the scribes and Pharisees because they are hypocrites.
- One time, Jesus tells us to forgive our enemies and to avoid violence. Another time, Jesus physically drives money changers out of the Temple with a whip, knocking over their tables in the process.
- One time, Jesus tells his disciples they should go out on their mission without money, extra clothes, or provisions. Another time, he tells them they should travel well-prepared, taking along extra money and extra clothes.

What's going on here? Is Jesus mixed up? Does he teach one thing and practice another? Not really. These examples just show that we can't take specific teachings and actions of Jesus in isolation and use them as "proof" for what is right and wrong. Instead, we have to see the "big picture." We have to see individual teachings and actions of Jesus in relation to his entire life.

Because it's easy to misinterpret individual Scripture passages and twist them to justify immoral actions, Jesus gave his Church a specific responsibility. The Church is the official interpreter of Jesus' moral teaching. It's the Church's job to help us understand Jesus' overall moral vision and apply it to specific moral problems. The Church has almost two thousand years of experience in doing this. Because of the Holy Spirit's guidance, the Church does a good job.

F.Y.I. ⑤

The moral teachings of Jesus are found throughout the Gospels and the Letters. The Sermon on the Mount, Matthew 5–7, summarizes many of Jesus' teachings on right living. Saint Paul, by his teaching and his letters, played a central role in helping the early Church understand and apply the moral teachings of Jesus.

3. Have the students gather in groups of four. Distribute a Bible to each group. Allow time for the groups to complete the **Scripture Search** activity on page **25**. Invite the groups to share with the class the prayer they composed.

4. Ask volunteers to take turns reading aloud the text, **More about Jesus**. Discuss as needed.

5. Ask another volunteer to read aloud the **F.Y.I.** section or allow time for the students to read this section silently on their own. Discuss as needed.

Optional

Tell the students that they can ask questions and receive information about Church teachings on-line. If your class has access to the Internet, help the students communicate with the Vatican Information Service (VIS) at http://www.vatican.va. By going into the News Net, the students can also find recent statements by the United States bishops and news of recent events in the Church all over the world.

Chapter Overview

The core of Jesus' moral teaching is not "how" to behave, but rather how good and precious each person is in God's eyes. This uniqueness does not lie in appearance, talents, or intelligence, but is rooted in inner qualities. Faith helps us see through externals and begin to value this inner worth of ourselves and others. Of course it isn't easy to see this inner goodness in people who, by appearance or behavior, don't seem to be worthy of our respect and concern. It's not easy to accept our own worth, either. But if we do begin to see with the eyes of faith, it becomes easier both to know and to do what is right in any given situation.

Scripture Background

The Sermon on the Mount is a collection of major teachings of Jesus. Make sure the students understand that Jesus is not saying we can wait for food and clothing to appear miraculously. We must work to provide for ourselves and others, but we must not let our work distract us from the love of God.

Materials
- Bibles

1. Have the students take turns reading aloud the first half of the section entitled **The Beatitudes** at the top of page **26**. Invite volunteers to share with the class their responses to the questions in the paragraph following the Scripture quotation from the Book of Matthew.

2. Allow time for the students to write their own definitions of the word *blessed* in the activity **You Define It**. Invite volunteers to share their responses.

3. Ask students to read the final two paragraphs of **The Beatitudes** at the bottom of page **26**. Make note of the words *harmony* and *freedom* and the explanation of their relationship.

4. Call attention to the **Catechism Connection**. Ask students to discuss the relationship between the present world and God's reign and how we might work for God's kingdom here and now.

Optional

Divide the class into small groups, and distribute magazines, scissors, and art materials. Ask each group to make a collage showing some of the types of people and actions that are mentioned in the Beatitudes—for example one person comforting another who is sad. When the groups have finished, call on them to show and explain their collages.

Materials

- magazines (optional)
- scissors (optional)
- art materials (optional)

The Beatitudes

Many of Jesus' moral teachings are found in the Sermon on the Mount. This Sermon begins with the Beatitudes. Jesus taught that these actions are *how* to be signs of God's reign. First, note that they are called *Beatitudes*. To experience the Beatitudes is to experience or to have blessedness, deep inner contentment, and well-being. Jesus is saying that if you do these things, you not only help bring about God's reign, you also experience real blessing.

When you first look at the Beatitudes, this sounds like a real contradiction. Here are the Beatitudes as found in the Gospel of Saint Matthew. Read it over carefully.

"Blessed are the poor in spirit, for theirs is the kingdom of heaven.

"Blessed are those who mourn, for they will be comforted.

"Blessed are the meek, for they will inherit the earth.

"Blessed are those who hunger and thirst for righteousness, for they will be filled.

"Blessed are the merciful, for they will receive mercy.

"Blessed are the pure in heart, for they will see God.

"Blessed are the peacemakers, for they will be called children of God.

"Blessed are those who are persecuted for righteousness' sake, for theirs is the kingdom of heaven.

"Blessed are you when people revile you and persecute you and utter all kinds of evil against you falsely on my account. Rejoice and be glad, for your reward is great in heaven, for in the same way they persecuted the prophets who were before you."

—Matthew 5:3–12

How can you be blessed when you are poor? Meek? In mourning, hungry and thirsty, persecuted? Shouldn't you try to avoid poverty, to stand up for your rights, to get even if someone wrongs you, to have enough to eat and drink, and to be popular? How can being meek, mournful, poor, or hungry possibly help bring about God's reign of justice and peace? What is Jesus really saying?

Give your definition of what it means to be *blessed* as a human being. Write it here.

_____

_____

_____

 There are a lot of different ideas about what it means to be blessed. A lot of people think being blessed equals wealth, power, or popularity. In the Beatitudes, Jesus doesn't define blessedness in terms of having things. For Jesus, being blessed is a question of having certain internal qualities, or attitudes.

The first of these qualities is an inner harmony—harmony with yourself, with your neighbor, with the material world, and ultimately, with God. The second quality is freedom. You're happy when you are free from the control of material things, the control of selfish impulses such as anger and revenge, the control of false values such as pride and popularity. Living the Beatitudes allows us to experience this harmony and freedom.

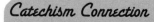

In the Lord's Prayer, "thy kingdom come" refers primarily to the final coming of the reign of God through Christ's return. [Cf. Titus 2:13.] But, far from distracting the Church from her mission in this present world, this desire commits her to it all the more strongly. (2818)

26

Resource Center

The Language of Faith

God's *reign* refers to an everlasting relationship of perfect justice, peace, and love between God and humanity. Although the reign of God will exist fully and perfectly only with the second coming of Christ, God has given the Church the special mission of proclaiming to all peoples on earth the kingdom of God established by Jesus. God has sent the Holy Spirit to help the Church fulfill this mission. As members of the Church, we are called to be a sign of God's presence in the world here and now.

Teaching Tip

Clarifying concepts Make sure the students understand this point: God alone has the power to bring about the kingdom. Our work on behalf of God's kingdom on earth is possible only if we respond to God's life-giving gift of grace.

The poor in spirit  ⑤

Look at the first Beatitude, "Blessed are the poor in spirit . . . ," as an example. Jesus isn't saying that blessedness depends on lacking the necessities of life: food, clothing, shelter, and so forth. Jesus is saying that real blessedness comes when you don't let material goods control you. You don't spend all your time worrying about how to get more goods or how to hang on to what you have. You are "poor in spirit" when you view material goods as a means to an end, not an end in themselves. You are "poor in spirit" when you believe helping other people is more important than getting rich. You are "poor in spirit" when you have enough faith to realize only God can provide all things.

"Therefore do not worry, saying, 'What will we eat?' or 'What will we drink?' or 'What will we wear?' For it is the Gentiles who strive for all these things; and indeed your heavenly Father knows that you need all these things. But strive first for the kingdom of God and his righteousness, and all these things will be given to you as well.

—Matthew 6:31–33

⑥ Class discussion.

Can you see how having this kind of attitude makes you blessed? Rather than being controlled by material things, you remain free. Rather than spending all your time worrying about what you might need, you are at peace, confident that God cares for you and knows what you need. Having the right attitude toward material goods puts you in harmony with the earth. You value material goods for their real purpose. You appreciate them. You enjoy them as God intends, but you don't make them "gods" and you don't let them enslave you.

If you aren't enslaved and totally dependent on having possessions, you are much more willing to share what you have with others. You don't worry that giving to others means less for yourself. In fact, the very act of sharing gives you a special experience of blessedness. It is something of a mystery, but it is true that if everyone were poor in spirit, there would be no poverty in the world! And that would be a blessed world. Each of the Beatitudes is like that. So let's take a quick look at each of the Beatitudes to see what they really mean.

5. Have the students take turns reading aloud **The poor in spirit** on page **27**.

6. Ask students to contrast the worldview described in the text with the acquisitive, materialistic attitude in America today. Ask: What factors contribute to this attitude? How can it be changed?

Optional

When people speak about treasure, they often mean gold. Invite interested students to find out more about gold—its properties, uses, location, how it is recovered and processed—and report their findings to the class.

27

Scripture Background

In *Matthew 6:21* Jesus explains the difference between earthly riches, which can be destroyed or stolen, and real treasure, those things from God that have lasting value. The word that Jesus used for wealth—*mammon*—comes from a Hebrew or Aramaic word meaning "that in which one trusts." Jesus cautioned against spending one's life acquiring material goods for security rather than trusting in and serving God.

Catechism Background

For more information about the Beatitudes and their relationship to Christian life, you may want to read the *Catechism of the Catholic Church* (#s 1716–29).

1. Ask for volunteers to take turns reading aloud **The meek, the merciful, and the peacemakers** on page **28**. Ask the students: What do these Beatitudes tell us about our relationship with others? *(that we should be in harmony with others)* How can you show confidence? *(by being humble, forgiving, and eager to reconcile with our enemies)*

2. Continue the discussion of the Beatitudes by having the students read **Those who mourn, hunger, and thirst**. Ask: If you are saddened by evil and injustice, what does that mean? *(that you are sensitive and aware, you hunger for what is right)* When will you be comforted? *(when you work for a more just world and, ultimately, when God's reign comes)*

3. Draw the students' attention to the **F.Y.I.** on page **28**. Ask students to imagine what the world would be like if this statistic were reversed. Invite them to share their thoughts.

4. Allow time for the students to complete the **What in the World?** activity. Discuss as needed.

The meek, the merciful, and the peacemakers ①

These three Beatitudes, though distinct, are closely related. They all deal with being in harmony with others, rather than competing with others or trying to control them. Basically, these three Beatitudes explain that blessedness doesn't mix with aggression, force, or vengeance. Controlling, aggressive people are very frightened, suspicious of others, and are caught up in selfishness. Being unhappy, violent people go about spreading unhappiness by physically and emotionally harming others.

When you are humble, forgiving, and eager to help enemies become friends again, you show confidence. You trust others. You have control of your temper. Because you don't carry around a lot of anger and have no desire to harm anyone, others feel safe and secure when you are around. In short, you experience an inner harmony, and you spread that peace and gentleness wherever you go. That's what being blessed is all about. And that's why Jesus can say, "Blessed are the meek, the merciful, the peacemakers."

F.Y.I. ③

There is one soldier for every forty-three people in the world but only one doctor for every one thousand people.

Those who mourn, hunger, and thirst ②

These two Beatitudes, more than most of the others, seem to go against the popular idea of what it means to be blessed. Ask people who have lost a family member or people who are hungry if their loss or hunger makes them feel blessed. They'll say "No way!" So how can Jesus say you'll be blessed if you mourn and experience hunger?

If the evil and injustice you see are what is making you sad, it means two things. First, rather than being trapped in selfish concerns or caught up in trivial interests, you are sensitive and aware of the pain and suffering of others. As a result, you hunger and thirst for what is right, for justice, for peace, for restoring fairness and harmony and order in society. This hunger moves you to try to create a more just world. Understanding God's call for justice provides a feeling of inner peace and blessedness even though you may continue to "mourn and hunger" (and work) for justice until God's reign is finally established. So Jesus is saying, "Blessed are those who mourn for the right reason and hunger for God's reign." Ultimately, they will be comforted and satisfied when that reign comes.

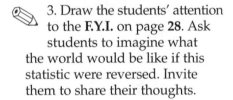

④ What in the World?

Try to name any TV shows, movies, or popular songs that promote the kinds of values contained in the Beatitudes. After each show, movie, or song, write the value it promotes. Compare your list with those of the others in your group.

TV show, movie, or song	Beatitude value

Resource Center

Scripture Background

Some of the Beatitudes are easy to understand, while others may need explanation. "Poor in spirit" is an attitude of dependence on God for the things we need in order to live a healthy, simple life. "Mourning" is the capacity to share the sorrows of others "Meekness" refers to nonviolent strength. The "pure of heart" are those who seek the will of God before all else. All the Beatitudes refer to qualities or attitudes that Christians should strive to possess.

The pure of heart

(6)

Pure of heart is sometimes translated as "single-minded," and that gives a good insight into what Jesus is saying here. Have you ever heard the expression "me third"? Usually when a person uses that saying, he or she explains it like this: God is the first priority in my life; the needs of my family and friends (and other people) are my second priority; then I tend to my own needs. In other words, to be pure of heart means to be unselfish, to have your priorities straight, to have your values in order. You don't make winning a game, getting the highest grade, or having the best bike your main concern. These things are good, but they aren't more important than showing honor to God or helping a person in need. Put simply, being pure of heart actually means "having your head on straight." You are "in sync" with God and neighbor. Putting God and others first gives great joy. It's like the goodness you feel when you give someone a great birthday or Christmas present—only it lasts all year long.

F.Y.I.  (8)

The early Christian martyrs took Jesus at his word and gave up their lives in their pursuit of God's reign.

The persecuted

(7)

Throughout history, it seems that people who are involved in injustice are always angered by the people trying to promote justice. They tease and ridicule the just, trying to make them look foolish. If they have enough power they arrest, abuse, and sometimes even kill the just. Many of the psalms complain about how the unjust treat the just. How can you be happy when people tease you, ridicule you, or, as is happening in some countries, arrest and abuse you for pursuing justice?

If you get persecuted by unjust people, it is a clear sign that you are doing the right thing—that you love and hunger for justice and are trying to promote it and that God is with you in your struggle. In other words, if you are being persecuted, you already have the attitudes described in all the other Beatitudes. You are already blessed, which is one of the things that threatens and angers the unjust. Being persecuted can cause emotional and even physical pain, but it can't rob you of that inner peace and blessedness you already have from living the Beatitudes. "Blessed are you when they persecute you for doing right."

(9) Getting Practical

Try to name one practical action or situation that would apply to each Beatitude.

1. Blessed are the poor in spirit.

_____

2. Blessed are those who mourn.

_____

3. Blessed are the meek.

_____

4. Blessed are those who hunger and thirst for righteousness.

_____

5. Blessed are the merciful.

_____

6. Blessed are the pure in heart.

_____

7. Blessed are the peacemakers.

_____

8. Blessed are those who are persecuted for righteousness' sake.

_____

29

5. Ask the students: What do you think the phrase "me third" means? What do we usually hear or say? *(me first)*

6. Have students read the section on page **29** entitled **The pure of heart**. Discuss the students' earlier responses to the phrase "me third" in light of the explanation in the first paragraph.

7. Ask for volunteers to read aloud **The persecuted**. Invite the students to give examples of people in history who stood their ground in the face of injustice, steadfast in their beliefs (and many times suffered because of these beliefs).

8. Have the students read silently the **F.Y.I.** Discuss as needed.

9. Allow time for the students to complete the **Getting Practical** activity at the bottom of page **29**. Invite the students to share their responses.

Optional

Gather the students in eight small groups. Assign each group one of the eight Beatitudes. Instruct the groups to prepare a short skit in which people their age are called upon to live by the values of the beatitude assigned to them. Allow time for the groups to present their skits for the class.

Chapter Overview

The Beatitudes seem to contradict our common sense, which says there is no connection between being happy and things such as poverty, persecution, hunger, and thirst. Properly understood, however, these inner attitudes are basic to what is ultimately necessary for happiness.

Background

The Beatitudes: Christians traditionally give the title *Beatitudes* to the eight teachings of Jesus presented in *Matthew 5:3–10*. The formula "Blessed is the one who . . ." occurs often in Old Testament wisdom literature; in using this style to describe the values of God's kingdom, Jesus was following a tradition familiar to his Jewish listeners.

1. Tell the students: Let's see what happens when we live the Beatitudes. Give the students a few quiet minutes to read silently the section on page **30** entitled **As you sow**. Ask volunteers to point out the effects and results we can expect from living the Beatitudes.

 2. Draw the students' attention to the **F.Y.I.** on this page. Ask if students know who Saint Ignatius Loyola was. *(founder of the Jesuits)* Have available a variety of books on saints for the students to look up a synopsis of Saint Ignatius Loyola's life. From his quote, what does Saint Ignatius Loyola want us to do?

 3. Draw the students' attention to the **Catechism Connection**. Ask the students why they think that Jesus gave the Church the responsibility of interpreting Scripture. What would happen if every person who read the Bible interpreted it the way he or she thought was right?

As you sow

Jesus mentions some of the specific effects of possessing and living out these Beatitude attitudes, such as:

- life in God's kingdom,
- inheriting the earth's good things for themselves and for always,
- experiencing comfort, mercy, fullness, and contentment,
- being true children of God, and
- seeing or understanding God.

Living the Beatitudes is the very way to obtain all God's blessings. If you are poor in spirit and are generous to others, you can be sure God will treat you the same way. You will never lack for basic necessities. If you turn the other cheek, show mercy, and offer forgiveness, you can be sure God will treat you the same way. If you focus on what is really important by being pure of heart, you will experience the very presence of God in your life.

By "losing your life" you actually gain it. If you give your life to Christ and his ways, you gain everlasting peace and life. Working for justice and peace, then, isn't so much one duty among others; working for justice and peace is what life is all about. Living justly and peacefully is what it means to be a disciple of Jesus and a child of God.

Pray as if everything depended on God; work as if everything depended on you.

—Saint Ignatius Loyola

Catechism Connection

. . . "Sacred Scripture must be read and interpreted in the light of the same Spirit by whom it was written." [DV 12§3.] (111)

30

Materials

- books on saints

Resource Center

The Language of Faith

Jesus gave us the *Beatitudes* in his Sermon on the Mount. The list of Beatitudes is not exhaustive; that is, Jesus did not list every possible group that will enter God's kingdom. Instead, Jesus pointed out a few groups. After giving the Beatitudes to the crowd who followed him, Jesus told them, "You are the light of the world." Jesus showed them the way to the Kingdom of God so that they in turn could show others.

Teaching Tip

Clarifying concepts To help students become more mature in their moral decision making, point out that the reward Jesus promises us for following the Beatitudes is not restricted to heaven in the future. Living the Beatitudes gives us and others real happiness now.

Scripture Search ④

Form a group with three other people. Assign one of the following passages in the New Testament to each group member. Summarize what the passage tells us about the moral teaching of Jesus. Then discuss what the passages are about. Write your notes in the space provided.

- Matthew 5:13–26

  We must follow God's commandments and teach others to do the same. We must make amends with those whom we are angry.

- Matthew 5:27–48

  We are to be faithful in our relationships and our promises. We must love our enemies and forgive and pray for those who have hurt us.

- Matthew 6:1–18

  God sees what we do in private and he will reward us. We must not actively seek praise when doing good deeds.

- Matthew 6:19–34

  We must not be a slave to our possessions and to money. We should not worry for God provides us with the things we need.

- Matthew 7:1–12

  We should not judge others for we will be judged by God. We must treat others as we want them to treat us.

- Matthew 7:13–29

  Jesus tells us that we may encounter obstacles as we follow the road to the kingdom of God. Only those who obey God and his commandments will be allowed to enter.

- Matthew 22:34–40 and John 13:34

  What we do for others is also what we do for Jesus. We are to love others as Jesus has loved us.

- Luke 6:20–49

  Jesus presents the greatest commandment.

- Ephesians 5:1–20

  We are to imitate God and live in love.

Scripture Background

James 4:17 reminds the community that Christian morality is based on a right relationship with God. We are presumptuous when we think we do not need God's help to do the right thing and to be happy. Such presumption leads to sin. We are not to judge others as if we ourselves were perfect. We all fail, at one time or another, to do the right thing.

4. Distribute Bibles and have the students form groups of four. Allow time for the groups to complete the **Scripture Search** on page **31**. Discuss as needed.

Optional

Review with the students chapter 2. Lead the students to see that sharing in Jesus' kingship means acting justly. Underlying the Church's teaching on social justice are six principles, which you may wish to discuss with the students: (1) All people are made in God's image and have dignity. (2) All people have individual rights and responsibilities. (3) All people are called to participate in community life and contribute to the common good. (4) Work is an expression of human dignity; all workers have rights. (5) All people have a special duty to help those who are poor. (6) Everyone in the world is our brother or sister.

Materials

- Bibles

1. Have the students remain in their groups of four. Direct them to the activity at the top of page **32**. Allow time for the groups to compose a short "sermon" that Jesus might preach in church today. When everyone is finished, ask a representative from each group to share with the class the group's sermon.

 2. Allow time for the students individually to complete the **Journal** entry.

3. Ask volunteers to take turns reading aloud the text, **God's love**. Discuss the text by asking the students these questions:

- Why do all people have dignity? *(Because all people are created good by God and are loved by God.)*

- Why does morality begin when we start loving ourselves? How is healthy self-love different from being selfish?

- What do you think is God's plan for the world? Why do you think this?

- What could you say to a friend who is depressed that might help him or her really feel God's love?

 4. Ask another volunteer to read aloud the **F.Y.I.** section or have the students read it silently on their own. Discuss as needed.

 5. Draw the students' attention to the **Catechism Connection**. Perhaps have the students take a moment or two of silence to "be" in God's presence and to get in touch with God's love for them.

Optional

Have the students think about times when family members or friends have been signs of God's love to them. Invite the students to write letters of thanks to those people. Encourage them to deliver their letters.

---

① As a group, write a short "sermon" that Jesus might preach in church today. Write an appropriate title. Then summarize in twenty-five words or less the moral teaching of Jesus. Use a separate piece of paper for your rough draft. Then write your group's final version here:

Title: _____

Sermon: _____

_____

_____

_____

_____

② Here is one way I will put on the mind and heart of Jesus this week:

_____

_____

_____

God's love ③

As the Church tells us, the morality of Jesus is based on his faith in *Abba*, his loving Father. That's the "bottom line." Jesus believed that all people are created in his Father's image and have dignity because God loves them. God loves the poor as well as the rich, people who are ill as well as people who are healthy, the old as well as the young, prisoners as well as law-abiding citizens.

So what does God's love mean in terms of morality? Simply this: Morality based on faith begins when you love God, love yourself the way God loves you, and love others as yourself.

Most likely you've heard this all before: "You're unique." "You're special." "There's no one in the world quite like you." But it's hard to feel unique and special if you get average grades, have average height, have average looks, and have the same talents that most of your classmates have.

But still Jesus says that each person is special. When he says this, he's looking beyond the things you see in yourself—your hair color, weight, inability to do math, or reluctance to practice the piano. Jesus says that you make a difference to God! God's plan for the world includes you! God is proud of you, just as parents have a special pride in each of their children. It has nothing to do with appearances or accomplishments or talents. God loves you.

Think about it: Your parents probably loved you and bragged about you when all you could do was lie in your crib. They didn't have to wait to begin loving you until you got a straight A report card or won some award. Well, God feels the same way toward you. God isn't waiting for you to do something the world considers great. You're great already in God's eyes. God is calling you to respond to his covenant of love.

F.Y.I.  ④

In your brain alone, you have over two billion individual cells. You are indeed a very special creation!

Catechism Connection ⑤

Our moral life has its source in faith in God who reveals his love to us. . . . (2087)

32

Resource Center

Link to Justice

Remind the students that one step in loving our neighbor is forgiving those who wrong us. Have the students stand in a circle and rest one hand in the other, palms up. Tell the students to think about a wrong that was done to them in the past and then imagine that wrong resting in their palms. Explain that when we forgive someone we release the wrong and the anger or disappointment that goes with it so there is room again for love. Ask the students to lift their hands and symbolically blow the wrong from their palms. Then have them join hands with their classmates as you lead them in praying, "Lord, we forgive to make room for your love. Amen."

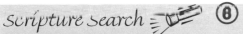 *Scripture Search* **⑧**

Read the following Scripture passages. Summarize them in your own words. Then discuss with the class what the passages are about.

- Isaiah 41:8–10
  We have been called to be God's own; God is always with us.

- John 3:16–21
  God's own Son, Jesus, is proof that God loves us.

- John 15:9–10
  Jesus loves us just as God loves him.

⑦

How the world would be different without me:

Here are some things I love about myself:

I believe God loves me and sees me as special because:

33

---

 6. Distribute Bibles and have the students work alone to complete the **Scripture Search**. As a class, discuss the meaning of each Scripture passage.

7. Allow time for the students to answer the three **Journal** entries on page **33**.

Optional

To highlight some of the ways in which each of us is biologically unique, talk about the fact that everyone has unique fingerprints. Have the students use a ink pad to "stamp" their thumb prints for comparison. You may also want to introduce the idea that studies involving DNA point to the unique genetic makeup of each individual.

Optional

Invite the students to think of an activity that they can do together as a sign of God's love. You might suggest making greeting cards for residents of a shelter or care center, supporting a Giving Tree at Christians, or collecting canned goods for a soup kitchen. Allow the students some time to plan several different activities or a repeated activity for the year, which they can record on a class calendar.

Chapter Overview

The point of this chapter can easily be missed by young people. It can seem like so many words and so many clichés. But it is the basis for Christian morality. Take extra pains to help the students get beyond the words to the truth they convey: You are an incredibly wonderful person in God's eyes. So is everyone else! Act accordingly, and you fulfill all your moral responsibilities.

Teaching Tip

Clarifying concepts: Remind the students that God made each person to be different from other people and special in his or her own way. Emphasize that as part of God's creation, we are all worthy individuals whose lives have meaning in the context of community. God does not promise that life will be easy, but he does give all of us the tools to help us face challenges and grow and learn throughout life. Trusting in God to help us learn and grow is part of our journey of faith.

Materials
- Bibles
- ink pad (optional)

1. Ask volunteers to take turns reading aloud the text, **Your neighbor as yourself.**

2. Divide the class into small groups. Allow a specified amount of time for each group to create a role-play of a typical "problem" situation involving junior high students and parents, friends, teachers, and so forth. The groups should develop two solutions to the situation in the role-play—one that does not use the law of love and one that does. At the end of the allotted preparation time, have each group present its role-play problem and solutions for the class. Discuss as needed.

 3. Ask another volunteer to read aloud the **F.Y.I.** section, or have the students read this section on their own. Ask: "What would your life be like if everyone around you lived the law of love?" Discuss as needed.

 4. As a class, discuss the two **Something to talk about** questions. Encourage as many students as possible to participate in the discussion.

5. Ask volunteers to take turns reading aloud the text, **Human goodness.**

 6. Conduct a whole-class discussion of the two **Something to talk about** questions.

7. Distribute drawing paper, glue, crayons, markers, scissors, and magazines. Allow time for the students to work (either alone or in small groups) on one of the suggested activities.

Materials

- art supplies

---

① **Your neighbor as yourself** ② *Role-play activity.*

For the sake of argument, let's suppose you believe that God truly loves you. Now listen to Jesus' interpretation of the Golden Rule, the basis of all his moral teaching: "Love your neighbor as you love yourself." that innocent-sounding rule, which you've probably heard a million times already, takes on a whole new meaning.

You deserve to have a deep, strong, confident love for yourself because of the goodness God sees in you. But so does your neighbor! So does every other kid in the class. So does the "enemy" who bugs you on the school bus, the funny-looking kid that everybody teases, and the crossing guard who is always crabby.

It's just common sense that you should love (that is, treat fairly and kindly) the members of your own family, your close friends, and the important people in your life. But faith takes us way beyond that. Faith gives us new eyes. Faith lets us recognize *everyone* as our neighbor.

Furthermore, faith helps us realize that every person in this world has dignity and deserves just treatment. Each person is special in the eyes of God. Each person, even though we don't know his or her name, deserves our respect and concern. Each person is a unique child of God. This person is family.

F.Y.I. ✏️ ③

"See how they love each other" was the way Romans used to talk about the early Christians. Apparently the Christians took seriously the command to "love your neighbor."

SOMETHING TO TALK ABOUT ④

1. What are some things that keep people from living Jesus' law of love?

2. What can we do to remind ourselves that every person is special?

Human goodness ⑤

Morality built on faith requires true love for yourself. You need to believe in your own goodness—the goodness God has given you and sees in you—before you can discover the real goodness, the specialness every other person has. God has shared with us his very life and love. As God's children, we have been given everything we need to respond with love toward God and others.

Here's some good news. Once you have enough faith to love yourself and to believe in the goodness others really have, "being good" is a lot simpler. You more or less instinctively know the right thing to do; it's easier to carry through and do what you should do. You *do* good because you know you (and others) *are* good.

This takes time to sink in. But that's what needs to happen if you're going to continue on your journey toward moral maturity. So we're going to spend a little more time with Jesus' kind of morality in the next chapter. Meanwhile, think about this: Jesus didn't teach us how to be good; Jesus taught that we are good.

SOMETHING TO TALK ABOUT ⑥

1. Why do you think it can be so hard to believe that you are unique and special to God?

2. How would you explain to others the statement "Jesus didn't teach us how to be good; he taught us that we are good"?

⑦ **Activity**

Make a collage, draw a picture, or write a poem that expresses the goodness of all people, including yourself.

34

Resource Center

Scripture Background

Luke 10:27, often referred to as the Great Commandment, is based on *Deuteronomy 6:5* and *Leviticus 19:18*. This commandment is also found in other Gospels. It reminds us that loving God, our neighbor, and ourselves leads to eternal life. According to Luke's Gospel a lawyer asks Jesus this question: "What must I do to inherit eternal life?" Jesus responds with the Great Commandment. Later, when the same lawyer asks Jesus to explain what *neighbor* means, Jesus responds with the parable of the Good Samaritan, which teaches us that everyone is our neighbor, regardless of ethnic background, religion, or nationality. It is important to be a neighbor rather than to judge who does and who does not deserve our help.

 **Gather for prayer.**

Reflection

 "I give you a new commandment, that you love one another. Just as I have loved you, you also should love one another. By this everyone will know that you are my disciples, if you have love for one another." (John 13:34–35)

10 Share your collage, picture, or poem. Briefly discuss ways that young people can help one another believe in God's love for them.

11 Here is one way I will help someone else feel God's love this week:
_____
_____
_____

12 *Jesus,*
Help me accept and work with the gift of faith you have given me.
Help me, through the eyes of faith, recognize you in each person I meet.
Help me realize how much God loves me so that I can love others and believe in their goodness.
Amen.

35

8. Gather the students, with their books, a pen/pencil, and artistic creation (step 7) in the designated prayer corner or sacred space. If fire laws permit, light a candle.

9. After the students have become settled, ask a student to read John 13:34–35 (page **35**). Invite the students to reflect silently on what they have heard.

10. After a brief period of silence, ask volunteers to share their collage, picture, or poem. Then have the students discuss ways that young people can help one another believe in God's love for them.

 11. Allow time for the students to complete the **Journal** entry.

12. Pray together the prayer.

Optional

Conclude the **Reflection** by listening to or by singing an appropriate song.

- "Dwelling Place" by John Foley from *Glory & Praise* (OCP [NALR]), *Gather (Comprehensive)* (GIA).

- "We Are God's Work of Art" by Marty Haugen from *Gather (Comprehensive)* (GIA).

- "We Walk by Faith" by Marty Haugen from *Gather (Comprehensive)* (GIA).

Link to Language Arts

Read aloud the following description of human interconnectedness written by clergyman and poet John Donne: *No man is an island, entire of itself. . . . Any man's death diminishes me, because I am involved in mankind; and therefore never send to know for whom the bell tolls; it tolls for thee.* Ask the students what they think this passage means and what it has to do with the text on this page. *(We are all related, all human; we are all affected by what happens to others.)* Invite the students to make up advertising slogans that convey the idea that we are not alone. You might offer these examples: "The world from A to Z"; "Me and you, you and me"; and "We are all part of one story that began with God's glory." Challenge pairs of students to create their own slogans.

1. Remind the students to do the **Homework** and to review the chapter for the next class.

Optional

There will be a short quiz at the beginning of the next class.

Multimedia Resources

Jesus In My Life Today, produced by Robert Blaskey (video) (BROWN-ROA, 1-800-922-7696).

Stories of the Human Spirit, "The Fasting Monk," produced by ACTA Publications (video) (BROWN-ROA, 1-800-922-7696).

Stories of the Human Spirit, "The Helper and the Homeless Woman," produced by ACTA Publications (video) (BROWN-ROA, 1-800-922-7696).

The Challenge of the Beatitudes, produced by ROA Media (video) (BROWN-ROA, 1-800-922-7696).

The Cleansing of the Temple (video) (BROWN-ROA, 1-800-922-7696).

Together in Faith, produced by Salt River Production Group (video) (BROWN-ROA, 1-800-922-7696).

HOMEWORK   ①

Scripture Puzzle

Look up the following verses and fill in the blanks. Then locate the words in the word search.

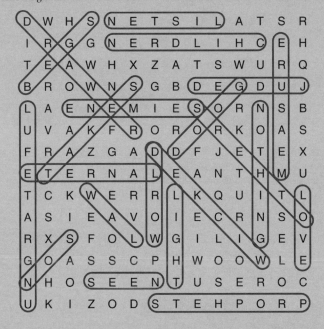

Matthew 7:1–2, 12 "Do not judge, so that you may not be _____. For with the judgment you make you will be judged, and the _____ you give will be the measure you get. . . . In everything do to _____ as you would have them do to you; for this is the _____ and the _____."

Luke 6:27, 30, 35 "But I say to you that _____, Love your _____, do _____ to those who hate you. . . . Give to everyone who _____ from you; and if anyone _____ away your goods, do not ask for them again. But _____ your enemies, do good, and lend, expecting _____ in return. Your _____ will be great, and you will be _____ of the Most High; for he is kind to the _____ and the _____."

John 3:16, 21 "For God so loved the _____ that he gave his only _____, so that everyone who believes in him may not perish but may have _____ life. . . . But those who do what is true come to the _____, so that it may be clearly _____ that their deeds have been done in God."

36

Answers to the Homework

Matthew 7:1–2, 12 "Do not judge, so that you may not be judged. For with the judgment you make you will be judged, and the measure you give will be the measure you get. . . . In everything do to others as you would have them do to you; for this is the law and the prophets."

Luke 6:26, 30, 35 "But I say to you that listen, Love your enemies, do good to those who hate you. . . . Give to everyone who begs from you; and if anyone takes away your goods, do not ask for them again. But love your enemies, do good, and lend, expecting nothing in return. Your reward will be great, and you will be children of the Most High; for he is kind to the ungrateful and the wicked."

John 3:16, 21 "For God so loved the world that he gave his only Son, so that everyone who believes in him may not perish but may have eternal life. . . . But those who do what is true come to the light, so that it may be clearly seen that their deeds have been done in God."

3: The Bottom Line
Review Quiz

True or False

_____ 1. Faith gives us a different slant on morality.

_____ 2. The most obvious place to discover the mind and heart of Jesus is in the Old Testament of the Bible.

_____ 3. Jesus referred to God affectionately as Abba.

_____ 4. Jesus used the image of the reign of God to describe how we should live as a family.

_____ 5. Viewing others with the eyes of faith lets us see them as unique people in the eyes of God.

_____ 6. Morality based on faith begins with love for others.

Fill in the Blanks

1. Many of Jesus' moral teachings are found in the _____ in the beginning of the Sermon on the Mount.

2. Morality based on faith means putting on the _____ and _____ of Jesus.

3. _____ is the official interpreter of Jesus' moral teaching.

4. Jesus believed that all people are created _____ by God and have _____ because God loves them.

5. Jesus said, "Love your _____ as you love yourself."

6. If you are poor in spirit, you are not controlled by material things and you remain _____.

BROWN-ROA, a division of Harcourt Brace & Company

3: The Bottom Line
Review Quiz

Essay

1. Explain why it is important that the Church be the official interpreter of Jesus' moral teaching. What are some difficulties that develop if an individual person tries to do the interpreting?

2. To experience the Beatitudes is to experience blessedness, inner contentment, and well being. In some cases, the wording of the Beatitudes makes this seem like a contradiction. Select two of the Beatitudes and explain how they carry out their promise.

3. Explain how living a life of faith, following the moral teachings of Jesus in the Beatitudes, can help bring about the coming of God's kingdom.

BROWN-ROA, a division of Harcourt Brace & Company

A New Understanding

You owe it to yourself ③

If you truly have faith, you know that you are a unique and special child of God. You have a right to inherit all of the love and happiness that God possesses, both now and in eternity.

If this realization really sinks in, imagine the kind of self-respect that faith can give you. With faith, you don't need rules or commandments or fear of punishments to get you to act in the right way. All you need is to believe in how special and good you really are. This kind of believing gives you an inner sense of how important it is to care for yourself.

Indeed, the kind of morality that Jesus teaches starts with self-love and self-respect. Such love of self involves the following actions:

- Appreciating and respecting the body you possess (eating healthily, exercising, bathing regularly, getting enough sleep, etc.)
- Developing whatever talents you may have (playing a musical instrument, painting, singing, working with wood, etc.)
- Educating your mind (reading, thinking, solving problems, learning from others, etc.)

If you follow the morality of Jesus, you'll do these things—not because they're rules or because your parents and teachers climb all over you when you don't—but because you love yourself and want to respond to God's love.

Whenever you take the easy way out (and we all do sometimes) by not studying, by not eating right, or by not getting the kind of exercise you know you need, you are betraying yourself and God. Deep inside you know it. You know it because of faith.

Faith really doesn't add new rules to the commonsense rules you already know. Instead, faith gives you a new appreciation of you and of *God*, Father, Son, and Spirit.

F.Y.I. ✎ ④

Scientists tell us that we only use about 30 percent of our brain cells. Can you imagine what we could do if we operated at full capacity?

37

Chapter 3 Quiz Answers

True or False

1. T	4. T
2. F	5. T
3. T	6. F

Fill in the Blanks

1. Beatitudes	4. good, dignity
2. mind, heart (any order)	5. neighbor
3. The Church	6. free

Essay

1. The Church is the official interpreter of Jesus' moral teaching because it's easy to misinterpret individual Scripture passages and twist them to justify immoral actions. It's the Church's job to help us understand Jesus' overall moral vision and apply it to specific moral problems.

2. Responses may vary. Refer to pages 27–29 in the student book for a detailed discussion of each beatitude.

4

Lesson Procedure

Academic Goal: To understand that, in addition to healthy self-love, Christian morality includes love of God and love of everyone as our "neighbor."

Attitudinal Goal: To appreciate faith as an important component in morality.

1. Go over the chapter 3 **Homework** answers, found on page **36**.

2. Review chapter 3 by giving the students a quiz. Reproduce page **36A** and/or page **36B** and give one to each student. After the students have completed the quiz, collect them to correct later. If you wish, correct the quizzes in class with the students.

Optional

As the students take the review quiz, collect their textbooks and journals. Scan the pages to make sure the students are completing the **Journal** activities. Also scan for indications of problems that should be addressed.

3. Have the students take turns reading aloud **You owe it to yourself** on page **37**. Discuss as needed.

✎ 4. Ask a volunteer to read aloud the **F.Y.I.** section, or have the students read the section on their own. Discuss the **F.Y.I.** question.

1. Ask a volunteer to read aloud the first paragraph of **Sins against respect and love**.

2. Have the students form small groups and distribute at least one dictionary to each group. Allow time for the group members to complete the chart and to discuss their answers.

Optional

Ask the students to discuss smoking, illegal drug use, and alcohol consumption. What is right and what is wrong about each of these actions? How can they show a lack of self-respect?

Optional

Taking good care of our bodies is one important responsibility all of us have. Distribute art materials, and have the students work in small groups to make posters about good health habits. Display the posters in the classroom.

Sins against respect and love

When it comes to morality, the Catholic Church recognizes the importance of respect and love. Whenever we don't love, we are choosing what's wrong. In fact, we are sinning. The seven basic ways that people sin are called the *capital sins*. The word *capital* means "very wrong" and "very basic." Capital sins are the root of all other sins.

Here is a list of the seven capital sins. In a small group, find the definition of each word in the dictionary. Decide how each sin shows a lack of love or respect. Then discuss ways to avoid these sins and to grow in healthy love.

Pride How does this sin show a lack of respect?
_____
_____
What is one way to avoid this sin and to grow in healthy love?
_____

Greed How does this sin show a lack of respect?
_____
_____
What is one way to avoid this sin and to grow in healthy love?
_____

Lust How does this sin show a lack of respect?
_____
_____
What is one way to avoid this sin and to grow in healthy love?
_____

Anger How does this sin show a lack of respect?
_____
_____
What is one way to avoid this sin and to grow in healthy love?
_____

Gluttony or drunkenness How does this sin show a lack of respect?
_____
_____
What is one way to avoid this sin and to grow in healthy love?
_____

Envy How does this sin show a lack of respect?
_____
_____
What is one way to avoid this sin and to grow in healthy love?
_____

Laziness How does this sin show a lack of respect?
_____
_____
What is one way to avoid this sin and to grow in healthy love?
_____

38

Materials
- dictionaries
- art materials (optional)

Chapter 3 Quiz Answers (continued)

3. Jesus taught that the Beatitudes are how to be signs of God's reign. To experience the Beatitudes is to experience or to have blessedness, deep inner contentment, and well-being. Jesus is saying that if we do these things, we not only help bring about God's reign, we also experience real blessing.

Resource Center

Chapter Overview

Healthy self-love is both a proof and a result of faith. Genuine faith helps us discover just how special we and our gifts really are. But faith takes us in another direction, too. It takes us outside ourselves and our own little "group." It impels us toward love of others and love of God.

③ First thoughts

Write down the name of each of the groups listed below. After the name of each group, write down the first word or phrase you think of that describes that group. *Don't show your list to anyone.* Fold the paper and put it aside. We'll come back to it later.

- Irish
- Mexican Americans
- Native Americans
- Men
- Women
- Whites
- African Americans
- Jews
- Elderly
- Teenagers

Members of the group ④

Respect is both a proof and a result of faith. Genuine faith helps you discover just how special you and your gifts really are. But faith takes you in another direction, too. It takes you outside yourself and your own little "group."

Groups have always been a part of human history. In fact, humans need groups in order to survive. In ancient times before there were countries and nations, most people lived in extended family groups. Survival depended on group loyalty. People were expected to risk their lives to protect their fellow group members. It was always a terrible thing to steal a cow from another group member, to murder a group member, or to lie to a group member. In a way, it was like sinning against yourself. You needed the members of your group to survive so that you, too, could remain alive.

Each group had its own strict moral code. But that's where morality stopped. It would be perfectly okay to steal a cow or a horse from some other group. It was, oftentimes, even a good thing to do so. No one was expected to tell the truth to people from other groups. Killing members of other groups was often considered a sign of bravery and honor.

It was common in those days to think that people from other groups weren't even human.

F.Y.I. ⑤

Even in ancient times, one of the strictest Jewish laws was the law of hospitality. You were expected to offer food and shelter to the homeless traveler.

39

Scripture Background

James 4:17 reminds the community that Christian morality is based on a right relationship with God. We are presumptuous when we think we do not need God's help to do the right thing and to be happy. Such presumption leads to sin. We are not to judge others as if we ourselves were perfect. We all fail, at one time or another, to do the right thing.

Link to Justice

In their pastoral letter "Brothers and Sisters to Us," the United States bishops call *racism*—hatred and prejudice toward other people because of race—a sin. Discuss examples of racism that have occurred throughout the world. Make sure you convey, both in your words and your attitudes, that Christians are to treat all people with dignity.

Explain that justice involves treating people as individuals, not as stereotypes. All members of a certain race are not the same and should not be judged alike. Likewise, it is not just to judge a person on age, gender, physical ability, or country or origin. In God's eyes all people have worth and dignity.

3. Distribute sheets of theme paper. Direct the students to complete the **First thoughts** activity. Advise the students to be honest in what they write. Also assure them that their answers will be private.

4. Ask volunteers to take turns reading **Members of the group**. Ask the students these questions:

- In today's world, are there any advantages to belonging to a group? Are there any disadvantages?
- What happens if you don't belong to a group?
- Who makes decisions in a group?

5. Ask a student to read aloud the **F.Y.I.** section, or allow time for the students to read it silently on their own. Point out that hospitality to strangers was a way of reaching beyond one's group to others. It helped the Jewish people remember that other people also deserved respect.

Optional

Bring to class, or have students bring, newspaper stories that show examples of people being loyal to their group but showing violence to others, for example, tribal warfare in Africa, Israeli-Palestinian violence, IRA and Protestant tension in Northern Ireland, and so forth. What suggestions can you make for easing these tensions?

Materials

- theme paper
- newspaper stories (optional)

1. Ask a student to read the section entitled **Today's groups**. Discuss as needed.

2. Have the students form groups of three or four to complete the chart on page **40**. When all the groups are finished working, discuss the answers in class.

Optional

To enhance their appreciation of the diversity of people that God has created, have the students make a people collage. Provide poster board and a wide variety of old newspapers and magazines containing pictures of people of various races and cultures. Have the students work in small groups to select pictures for their collages. Display the collages on a bulletin board titled *All God's People*, and use them to remind the students that as part of God's creation, we are called upon to respect all people.

Materials
- poster board (optional)
- old newspapers and magazines (optional)
- glue (optional)

Today's groups ①

Because we live in more "civilized" times, it's easy to think that we're better or more moral. But think about it: Are groups really less important today than they were thousands of years ago? Doesn't a group mentality still influence our concepts of what's right and what's wrong, who has rights and who doesn't, who's worthwhile and who's not?

To answer these questions, complete the activity on this page. Work with two or three others to fill in the chart. Then discuss your answers with the class.

②

Modern situation	What groups are found here?	How do these groups see right and wrong?
The world		
Your town or city		
Your neighborhood		
Your school		
Other: _____		

40

Resource Center

Link to Justice

The Church teaches the discrimination against and exclusion of others based on their race, culture, gender, age, or economic status is sinful. In their 1980 document "Cultural Pluralism in the United States," the bishops of the United States reminded us that everyone is a member of the human family. Christians have an obligation to accept and include everyone.

Just look around

One kind of modern-day group, the clique, may be right in your own school. In a clique, insiders are usually kind to each other, help each other, and stick up for each other. They have "rules" for how to treat each other. If they don't follow these rules, the group "punishes" them. Clique members usually do not feel any responsibility to act the same way toward outsiders. In fact, they can often act cruelly to anyone who isn't "in." Cliques can come in many forms. A football team might be a clique. An honor society might be a clique. A college fraternity or sorority might be a clique. A lot depends on the attitudes of the group members.

Street gangs are another example of a modern-day group. Gang members often have a fierce loyalty to everyone who wears the gang colors. In order to protect their turf or to exert their superiority, gang members may routinely wage war against rival gang members or they may vandalize rival gang property. Sadly, violence and death may be a common occurrence.

Racial prejudice is another example of a modern-day group mentality. Racially prejudiced people tend to look down on people of other races. They may even hate them or treat them as defective or inferior.

Actually, most kinds of prejudice reflect a group mentality. For example, some people have very strong prejudices against homosexuals. They regard homosexuals as subhuman and don't feel that such people have any rights. It's one thing to be against homosexuality as an action, but that doesn't mean we shouldn't treat homosexual persons with the dignity and respect all people deserve.

Some other people have very strong prejudices about nominating a woman for president or allowing women to work in certain jobs. They regard women as less capable than men, as somehow inferior.

The problem with any type of prejudice is that it prevents people from seeing anything wrong when they are cruel or unjust to nongroup members. Ironically, many people caught up in group prejudice are generally *good* people. They're convinced that lying to others is wrong, that bullying others is wrong, and that cheating or stealing is wrong. But their group mentality (prejudice) gives them a very narrow idea of what "others" means. They are blind to the existence and the rights of nongroup individuals.

 To what group(s) do you belong?
_____
_____

How does your group(s) feel toward outsiders? How does your group(s) treat outsiders?
_____
_____
_____

41

3. Ask volunteers to take turns reading aloud the text, **Just look around**. Ask the students to give real-world examples of the following:

- Nationalism that is destructive.
- Racial prejudice.
- Prejudice toward homosexuals.
- Prejudice toward women or the elderly.

Optional

Have the students form small groups. Ask each group to think of a situation in which a group or clique makes a decision and one member does not go along with it. What happens? How does the group treat the person who stands alone? Have the students take turns being the one who disagrees while the others role-play clique members who stick together. Talk about the experience.

4. Allow time for the students to work individually to complete the two **Journal** entries.

Optional

Remind the students that our families are perhaps the most important group to which we belong. Ask them to make lists of one or two positive qualities about each family member. Suggest that they think of ways to help their family members have a good attitude about themselves. Then encourage the students to express appreciation for those positive qualities during a family meal or prayer time.

Chapter Overview

A group mentality, such as that found in most cliques and gangs, is a big obstacle to appreciating the dignity and worth of other people. Such a mentality often leads to prejudice against anyone who is not in our particular group. It tends to restrict our sense of moral obligation to people we perceive as friends and family.

Link to the Faith Community

Ask the students to reflect on how they include (or exclude) other students or people in their community who have disabilities. Have the students develop a list of questions that can help the Church and the school evaluate how they respond to the needs of physically challenged members. Suggest a few questions such as these: Is our church accessible to persons with disabilities? Is there at least one Mass in which sign language is used? How can we make sure to include students with physical limitations in school activities?

1. Ask students to take turns reading aloud **What is prejudice?** After the reading, ask these questions:

- What is prejudice? (Have the students underline in the text "Prejudice is a conviction . . . that doesn't have facts to back it up.")

- How do we become prejudiced?

- Why does prejudice hurt people? How is it unfair?

- What is an example of a prejudice that is harmful?

- What is an example of a prejudice that is not harmful?

What is prejudice?

Prejudice is a conviction about something or someone that doesn't have facts to back it up. We prejudge, or judge, before we have all the information. Prejudice is learned; we aren't born with prejudices. Usually we pick up prejudices as young children. We learn them from family, friends, and our social or ethnic groups. Prejudices are very difficult to change because we become so convinced they are true that we never bother to challenge them.

Some forms of prejudice are less harmful than others. You can have a positive prejudice toward something. For example, if your family owned an apple orchard, you would probably think everyone should eat apples and apple products. If your family owned an orange grove, however, you'd be singing the praises of oranges rather than apples.

Prejudice becomes ugly when we translate *different* to mean that the members of a particular group lack certain important human qualities, such as intelligence, honesty, responsibility, etc. Things become really ugly when we translate *different* as threatening. Safety, jobs, property, health, certain moral values, etc. are important to all people. No one person or group of people is more deserving than another.

Some of the most harmful prejudices are those we develop toward groups of people. "People on welfare are lazy" is a common example of prejudice. Laziness is a serious fault, and saying that every person on welfare is lazy is a serious accusation. Making general statements judging an entire group of people is prejudicial. Some people are lazy and some are poor. All lazy people are not poor; however, neither are all poor people lazy.

You can see the real harm of a prejudice when you start applying it to individuals. Suppose you have always heard that "people on welfare are lazy" and you have come to accept it as true. One day at the supermarket you find yourself in line behind a woman you know from church. You have always respected her. She is paying for her food with food stamps. Would you change your mind about her because of this? Perhaps she is ill or her husband died and she can't earn enough money to support her family. Would you change your attitude toward her because she is poor? Then why do people create attitudes toward people because they are poor or disabled or of a different race?

The bottom line is that victims of prejudice are "guilty until proven innocent." The result of prejudice toward people is always the same: It unfairly robs its victims of the basic respect they deserve as humans and children of God.

42

Resource Center

Link to the Faith Community

Ask the students to be aware, especially when participating in liturgy, of the living proof that God created a community of people of all races. Young and old, rich and poor, and strong and weak live together on earth and worship together as part of creation.

Catechism Background

For more information on respect for the human person and the equality and difference in people, you may want to read the *Catechism of the Catholic Church* (#s 1929–34).

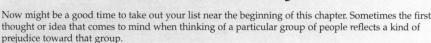

② Second Thoughts

Now might be a good time to take out your list near the beginning of this chapter. Sometimes the first thought or idea that comes to mind when thinking of a particular group of people reflects a kind of prejudice toward that group.

1. Review the words and phrases you listed after each group. Circle any that might reflect a possible prejudice—an opinion or attitude you have that you can't back up with facts or that you can't apply to everyone in that group. These can be positive or negative prejudices.

2. Where did you learn the opinion reflected in the words and phrases you circled?

3. Do you think you may have some prejudices you weren't aware of?

Love of neighbor ③

One of the most radical, revolutionary things Jesus taught attacks group prejudice at its roots. As Jesus explained, *neighbor* includes everyone. Jesus taught that enemies, public sinners, and foreigners are all our neighbors. Outcasts (the poor, the crippled, lepers, the insane, prisoners) are our neighbors, too.

Remember where Jesus is coming from. He sees *every human being* as a precious and unique child of God. Money, race, intelligence, religion, talents, or physical strength aren't what give people dignity. For Jesus, each person has dignity just by "being." For Jesus, there is only one group—the human race. So if you buy into Jesus' view of things, and if you begin to see others with the eyes of faith, then you begin to see and treat each person as a neighbor.

Here is a true story about one teenager who went beyond the group mentality and saw an outsider as Jesus does.

It's a cold winter day in Milwaukee. The bus stops and a pregnant woman of a minority race gets on. Her coat is thin and ragged. She smells bad, and she is barefooted. Most people on the bus just look away and pretend she's not there. But some high school kids in the back of the bus start making loud, insulting comments. They laugh and point at the woman's bare feet.

About three stops later, a fourteen-year-old boy, who is sitting alone, gets up to leave. He stops by the woman's seat and slips off his tennis shoes and socks. He hands them to the woman and says quietly, "Here, take these. I have another pair at home." Barefooted, he gets off the bus and heads down the street to his house.

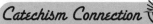

Catechism Connection ⑤

The duty of making oneself a neighbor to others and actively serving them becomes even more urgent when it involves the disadvantaged, in whatever area this may be. . . . (1932)

This same duty extends to those who think and act differently from us. The teaching of Christ goes so far as to require the forgiveness of offenses. . . . (1933)

SOMETHING TO TALK ABOUT ④

1. What kinds of group mentality (prejudice) are found in this story?

2. Why do you think most people on the bus ignored the woman?

3. Why did the high school kids laugh at her?

4. Why do you think the fourteen-year-old boy gave her his tennis shoes?

---

2. Direct the students to take out their theme papers (from page **39**) and complete the **Second Thoughts** activity. Again, stress to the students that their answers will be private.

3. Ask volunteers to take turns reading aloud the text on page **43**, **Love of neighbor**, and the accompanying story.

4. Have a class discussion of the four **Something to talk about** questions. Encourage all students to participate. Accept all reasonable answers.

5. Direct the students' attention to the **Catechism Connection**. Explain that all people are our neighbors. Because Jesus tells us to reach out to the disadvantaged, the Church has long been involved in programs that help minorities and new immigrants speak and read English, find jobs, and obtain decent housing.

Chapter Overview

Jesus' moral vision is revolutionary in that it breaks down the artificial barriers of the group mentality and helps us recognize each person as our neighbor no matter how society may judge that person.

Assessment Tip

Self-assessment: Use the following questions to help the students assess the degrees to which their actions reflect love. **When was the last time you shared food or drink with someone who was hungry or thirsty? When did you make someone feel welcome? When did you give clothes to someone in need? When did you visit or pray for someone who was sick? When did you talk with someone who was lonely?** Encourage the students to look for opportunities to demonstrate the law of love in their daily lives.

1. Draw the students' attention to the **Catechism Connection** on page **44**. Make sure the students realize that Christian morality reaches beyond the people we know and like to include even our enemies and total strangers.

2. Distribute Bibles. Have the students work individually on the **Scripture Search** activity on page **44**. When everyone has finished, discuss the passages as a class.

3. Divide the class into three or more groups. Assign each group one of the Scripture passages from the **Scripture Search** activity. Have the students prepare to retell their story in one of the formats listed in the **Activity** at the bottom of page **44**. Allow time for the groups to present their story.

Optional

Explain that the parable of the good Samaritan teaches that we are called to love and respect all people. Talk with the students about prejudice that exists today, and invite discussion about ways to overcome it.

Materials
- Bibles

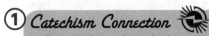

① Catechism Connection

. . . The Lord asks us to love as he does, even our enemies, to make ourselves the neighbor of those farthest away, and to love children and the poor as Christ himself. [Cf. Mt 5:44; Lk 10:27–37; Mk 9:37; Mt 25:40, 45.] (1825)

Scripture Search ②

In the time of Jesus, the Jews considered themselves to be chosen by God. They were a special group. Some of them had strong prejudices against people who did not follow the same religious laws. Some Jews were especially prejudiced against the Samaritans, their poor "cousins," who had intermarried with non-Jews. Samaritans, in turn, were prejudiced against Jews.

Read each of the following Scripture passages about Jesus' attitude toward Samaritans. Summarize Jesus' attitude in your own words and be prepared to talk about it with the class.

- Luke 10:29–37

  A good Samaritan goes out of his way to help a stranger.

- Luke 17:11–19

  Jesus cures ten lepers but only one returns to thank him.

- John 4:4–42

  Jesus breaches social custom to talk with a Samaritan woman.

③ Activity

Form a team to retell one of these Scripture stories for the class, using one of the following formats:

- Reading and pantomime
- Radio news broadcast
- Children's story
- TV talk show interview
- Rap-style poem

44

Resource Center

Chapter Overview

Our moral obligations also extend to God. Our relationship with God should involve praise and trust (the First Commandment), respect for God's dignity (the Second Commandment), and the inclusion of God as the center of our lives (the Third Commandment).

Art Background

"The Good Samaritan" was painted by Vincent van Gogh while he was hospitalized to restore his mental health. The parable tells of a Jewish man beaten by robbers and left to die until a compassionate Samaritan stopped. The traditional hostility between the Jewish people and the Samaritans made this a powerful gesture of love. Van Gogh's choice of subject was often deeply personal. Although this work is a "translation" of another painting by an artist he admired, it may be that van Gogh identified with the helpless victim.

What about God?

If needed, review the Ten Commandments (page 99).

We've seen how faith can give you a new sense of the responsibility you have to care for yourself and to respect others. But what about God? What responsibility do we have toward God? The answer lies in the first three commandments of the Ten Commandments. These commandments set up the ground rules for the respect we owe to God. Faith sharpens our understanding of these ground rules.

As you probably learned when you were younger, the first commandment is this: "I am the Lord your God. You shall not have false gods beside me." This commandment is about our moral obligation to praise and to trust God. The commandment also deals with idolatry. *Idolatry* means trusting creatures more than, or instead of, God. Idolatry means that we look for love, protection, and help from creatures because we don't trust that God loves us and will protect and help us.

Most people don't think the first commandment has anything to do with them. That's because they aren't into witchcraft and they don't worship animals or statues or the devil. But through faith, we begin to see that God deserves much more than we often give. We realize that maybe we do have "idols" we depend on more than we depend on God.

For example, some people worship money. Some people worship fame or popularity. Some depend on science to solve all their problems. Keep this straight: There's nothing wrong with money, popularity, or science. But when we depend more on these things for happiness than we trust that God loves us and seeks our happiness, then that's idolatry. Idolatry is morally wrong. It's a sin against God.

F.Y.I.

Another word for the Ten Commandments is the *Decalogue*. The Decalogue has similarities to other codes of law found in other countries at that time (around 1250 B.C.E.). Actually, the Ten Commandments are only the first part of a much more elaborate code, or covenant, that God formed with the Hebrews.

SOMETHING TO TALK ABOUT

What are some ways that young people today can obey the first commandment?

Here is one way I can praise and trust God:
_____
_____
_____

45

4. Ask volunteers to take turns reading **What about God?** on page **45**.

5. If necessary, review the Ten Commandments by having the students turn to page **99**.

6. Ask another student to read the **F.Y.I.** section, or allow time for the students to read this section on their own. Discuss as needed.

7. As a class, discuss the **Something to talk about** question.

8. Allow time for the students to work individually to complete the **Journal** entry.

Background

The Ten Commandments: Also known as the *Decalogue*, or "ten words," the Ten Commandments sum up the duties of the covenant relationship between God and his people.

Link to Justice

Explain to the students that prayer goes hand in hand with work for justice. Whenever we praise and adore God, we are giving God what is justly due him. When we pray for others, we are also giving to them what is due them, namely, our acknowledgment that God is the Creator of all people and that God's love is meant for all people to know and experience. By praying, we entrust others to the love and care of God.

1. Ask volunteers to take turns reading aloud **Two more ways to love God** on page **46**.

 2. As a class, discuss the two **Something to talk about** questions. Encourage all students to say something.

3. Allow time for the students to work individually to complete the two **Journal** entries.

4. Call on students to take turns reading aloud **Conscience, faith, and law**. Discuss as needed.

Two more ways to love God ①

The second and third commandments give us two more ways to love God.

The second commandment is this: "You shall not take the name of the Lord your God in vain." Some people think that this commandment is against swearing. While that is true, the commandment is also about our moral obligation to respect God. Because God is our Creator (indeed, the Creator of the entire universe), we should take God seriously.

Likewise, we have a moral responsibility to respect the things (churches, religious practices, bishops, priests, and other people who are dedicated to God's service) that are intended to give God special honor. Faith helps us see that respecting God is much more than not using his name in vain.

The third commandment is this: "Keep holy the Lord's day." As creatures made in God's likeness, we have a moral obligation to love and honor God as the center of our lives. Keeping holy the Sabbath means much more than attending Mass on Sundays when you understand it through the eyes of faith. It means continually working at your relationship with God through prayer and participation in the sacraments. It means associating with God on a day-to-day basis. It means including God in all that is important to you, just as you would include any good friend. Maybe that's the best way to summarize our responsibility to God. Be friends!

Conscience, faith, and law ④

There is usually a close connection between the Ten Commandments and the civil laws a government makes. For example, laws about speeding and drunk driving are related to the fifth commandment. Laws about false advertising and about lying under oath are related to the eighth commandment. Laws about vandalism, littering, and shoplifting deal with the seventh commandment. Laws about pornography, bigamy, and sexual abuse have to do with the sixth and ninth commandments.

Church laws are somewhat the same. They take the general moral values found in the Ten Commandments and the teachings of Jesus and translate them into specific practices for Catholics to follow. For example, the third commandment calls us to gather regularly as a community to worship God and to support each other. To help us carry out this commandment, the Church gives a more specific guideline or law: As a minimum, we are morally obliged to gather for Mass every Sunday and on certain holy days.

Civil laws may change from time to time, and they may vary from one country to the next. But their basic purpose remains the same: They intend to protect human rights. Likewise, some Church laws will change from time to time, but the ideas behind the laws remain the same. (For example, we can now worship together on either Saturday evening or on Sunday. Back in the 1950s, that wasn't the case. People had to go to church on Sunday morning.)

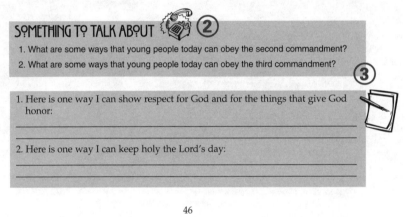

SOMETHING TO TALK ABOUT ②

1. What are some ways that young people today can obey the second commandment?

2. What are some ways that young people today can obey the third commandment?

③

1. Here is one way I can show respect for God and for the things that give God honor:

_____

_____

2. Here is one way I can keep holy the Lord's day:

_____

_____

_____

46

Resource Center

The Language of Faith

The word *worship* comes from an Old English word meaning "honor." Worship includes all the many ways we praise, thank, and revere God, especially as a community.

Scripture Background

In *Exodus 31:13*, God tells Moses that the Israelites must keep the Sabbath as a sign that they are a chosen, holy nation. This commandment is also meant to remind the Israelites of the seventh day of creation, when God rested. The Church asks us to honor this commandment by devoting Sunday to the worship of God and to activities that refresh us in body and spirit, strengthen our relationships with family and friends, or serve the needs of the community.

⑤ 7 8 ⑤ ACTIVITY 3 ⑥ 10

Form a group with three or four others. Work together to think of an example of the following laws. Then try to decide which commandment the law deals with. When you're finished, share your answers with the class.

Type of law	Example	Commandment
Civil		
School		
Family		

⑥ *Gather for prayer.* *Reflection*

⑦ *Love does no wrong to a neighbor; therefore, love is the fulfilling of the law. (Romans 13:10)*

⑧ Briefly discuss some practical ways that young people can love themselves, their neighbors, and God.

Here is one practical action I will take this week to love myself:
_____
_____

Here is one practical action I will take this week to love my neighbor:
_____
_____

Here is one practical action I will take this week to love God:
_____
_____

⑩ *Jesus,*
Help me trust God and realize that I am God's unique, special child.
Help me appreciate and develop my gifts in gratitude to God.
Help me not get involved in cliques or be drawn away from you and your love.
Amen.

47

---

5. Divide the class into groups of four or five. Allow time for the groups to complete the **Activity** chart on page **47**. When everyone has finished, call on each group to share its answers with the class.

6. Gather the students, with their books and a pen/pencil, in the designated prayer corner or sacred space. If fire laws permit, light a candle.

7. After the students have become settled, ask a volunteer to read Romans 13:10 (page **47**). Invite the students to reflect silently on what they have heard.

8. After a brief period of silence, ask the students to discuss practical ways that young people can love themselves, their neighbors, and God.

9. Allow time for the students to complete the **Journal** entries.

10. Pray together the prayer.

Optional

Conclude the **Reflection** by listening to or by singing an appropriate song.

- "Bring Forth the Kingdom" by Marty Haugen from *Gather (Comprehensive)* (GIA).
- "Turn to Me" by John Foley from *Glory & Praise* (OCP [NALR]).

Chapter Overview

As the students will learn, there is usually a close connection between the Ten Commandments and the civil laws a government makes. Civil and Church laws serve as a positive guide in applying general, moral principles contained in the commandments and the gospel. Specific laws may change from time to time, but the underlying principle of those laws—the protection of human rights—remains the same.

Scripture Background

In *Matthew 5:19*, which is part of the Sermon on the Mount, Jesus affirms the need for his followers to obey the commandments. Jesus expected his followers, with the aid of God's grace, to live the commandments in their hearts as well as express them in outward signs of obedience. As followers of Jesus today, we are expected not just to know the commandments but to follow them in our daily lives.

1. Remind the students to do the **Homework** and to review the chapter for the next class.

There will be a short quiz at the beginning of the next class.

Multimedia Resources

A Case of Conscience: Dealing with Peer Pressure, produced by Robert Blaskey (video) (BROWN-ROA, 1-800-922-7696).

Love, the Main Ingredient, produced by the Archdiocese of St. Paul-Minneapolis (video) (BROWN-ROA, 1-800-922-7696).

Moses the Lawgiver, produced by Rabbit Ears Production, Inc. (video) (BROWN-ROA, 1-800-922-7696).

Stories of the Human Spirit, "Junk," produced by ACTA Publications (video) (BROWN-ROA, 1-800-922-7696).

Street Hockey Hassle, produced by Twenty-Third Publications (video) (BROWN-ROA, 1-800-922-7696).

Swim Team Splash, produced by Twenty-Third Publications (video) (BROWN-ROA, 1-800-922-7696).

The Commandments, produced by ROA Media (video) (BROWN-ROA, 1-800-922-7696).

HOMEWORK ①

Use the following words from this chapter to complete in the fill-in puzzle on the next page.

Three Letters
God
owe

Four Letters
body
care
code
envy
love
lust
mind
self
sins
soul

Five Letters
anger
faith
gangs
greed
group
heart
human
Jesus
pride
rules
trust

Six Letters
church
clique
family
others
values

Seven Letters
capital
enemies
respect
talents
worship

Eight Letters
gluttony
idolatry
laziness
Lord's Day
morality
neighbor

Nine Letters
Decalogue
happiness
mentality
prejudice

Ten Letters
Samaritans

Eleven Letters
drunkenness

Twelve Letters
commandments

Fourteen Letters
responsibility

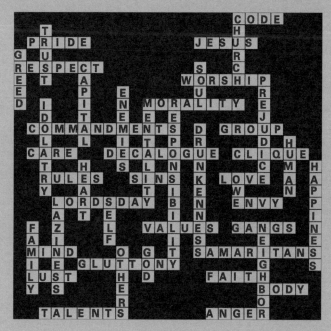

4: A New Understanding

Review Quiz

True or False

____ 1. Every person is a unique and special child of God.

____ 2. There are eight capital sins.

____ 3. The first three commandments define our moral responsibility toward God.

____ 4. Keeping holy the Sabbath only means getting to Mass on Sunday.

____ 5. Civil laws and religious laws have no connection.

____ 6. Some Church laws will change from time to time, but the idea behind the laws never changes.

Fill in the Blanks

1. The kind of morality that Jesus teaches starts with _____.

2. _____ doesn't add new rules to the commonsense ones you already know; it gives you a new appreciation of yourself.

3. _____ prevents people from seeing anything wrong when they are cruel or unjust to nongroup members.

4. Jesus taught that enemies, public sinners, and foreigners are all our _____.

5. The First Commandment is about our moral obligation to _____ and to _____ God.

6. Whenever we depend more on money, popularity, or science than we depend on God for our happiness, we commit the sin of _____.

BROWN-ROA, a division of Harcourt Brace & Company

4: A New Understanding
Review Quiz

Essay

1. Name the capital sins and tell why it is important to study and know them.

2. Explain how observing the commandments can help us carry out our responsibilities toward God and toward our neighbors.

3. Show how prejudice is behind many of the problems in our country and in our world today. How can you overcome prejudice in yourself and help others overcome prejudice in themselves?

5 **Freedom to Choose**

③ 🔔 **What is freedom?** ☀️

With two or three classmates, discuss your understanding of freedom. What words come to mind when you think of the word *freedom*? Write the group's words here:

_____
_____
_____

As a group, decide how you would define *freedom*. Write your definition here:
Freedom is _____
_____
_____
_____

Now look up the word *freedom* in a dictionary. What is the definition?
Freedom is _____
_____
_____
_____

Do you want to revise your group's definition? If so, rewrite it here:
Freedom is _____
_____
_____
_____
_____

④ SOMETHING TO TALK ABOUT

1. How are young people in our society free?
2. How are young people not free?
3. Do you think young people should be free to do anything they want? Why or why not?

⑤

How I am free:
_____

How I am not free:
_____

How I feel about the amount of freedom I have at this time in my life:
_____
_____

49

Chapter 4 Quiz Answers

True or False

1. T	4. F
2. F	5. F
3. T	6. T

Fill in the Blanks

1. self-love	4. neighbors
2. Faith	5. praise, trust (any order)
3. Prejudice	6. idolatry

Essay

1. The seven capital sins are pride, greed, lust, anger, gluttony or drunkenness, envy, and laziness. It's important to study and know the capital sins because they are the root of all other sins.

5

Lesson Procedure

Academic Goal: To understand the nature of human freedom, the ways freedom can be limited, and freedom's relationship to moral responsibility.

Attitudinal Goal: To take seriously the freedom and responsibility we now have to direct our own lives.

1. Go over the chapter 4 **Homework** answers, found on page **48**.

2. Review chapter 4 by giving the students a quiz. Reproduce page **48A** and/or page **48B** and give one to each student. After the students have completed the quiz, collect them to correct later. If you wish, correct the quizzes in class with the students.

Optional

As the students take the review quiz, collect their textbooks and journals. Scan the pages to make sure the students are completing the **Journal** activities. Also scan for indications of problems that should be addressed.

3. Have the students form small groups. Distribute dictionaries and have the groups complete the **What is freedom?** activity. If time permits, call on the groups to share their definitions of *freedom*. Perhaps reach a class consensus on what freedom is.

 4. As a class, discuss the three **Something to talk about** questions. Encourage everyone to participate.

 5. Allow time for the students to work alone to complete the **Journal** entries.

Materials

• dictionaries

1. Ask students to take turns reading aloud **Freedom and liberty** on page **50**. Discuss as needed.

 2. Ask a volunteer to read aloud the **F.Y.I.** section, or have the students read the section on their own.

Optional

Divide the class into small groups to create a role-play situation that illustrates the difference between freedom and liberty. The situations should be different from the examples given in the textbook. Allow time for the groups to present the role-plays. Discuss as needed.

Freedom and liberty

Young people often want more freedom. Actually, what they are really asking for is more liberty. Freedom and liberty are not the same thing. Freedom is the capacity to choose. This capacity is given to us by God. Freedom, like intelligence, is a spiritual power that can't be taken away from us without actually destroying who we are.

Liberty, on the other hand, is the ability to carry out the choices we make. This ability can be taken away from us without destroying who we are.

For example, prisoners in jail have lost their liberty to come and go freely. But their moral freedom remains intact. They remain free to choose the attitude they have in prison, the way they behave toward others, and how they spend their recreational time. They can choose to better themselves educationally and to reform their lives. Or they can choose to become hardened in crime. (Prison is intended, however, to prevent criminals from acting out this last choice!)

Here's another example: Across the United States, the law gives people age twenty-one and older the *liberty* to drink alcohol. But this does not mean that adults *have* to drink. They are free to choose not to drink. They are also free to decide how many drinks they will have if they do decide to drink.

Why is it important to know the distinction between freedom and liberty? It's important because being morally good depends on how we use our freedom, not our liberty. Morality depends on the choices we make with our freedom, whether or not we have the liberty to carry out those choices.

Here's an extreme example: Suppose Joe hates his parents and decides that he's going to kill them. He plans the murders but, when it comes time to carry them out, something goes wrong. (The gun doesn't fire; the poison doesn't work, etc.) He doesn't actually kill his parents. Nevertheless, he's *morally* wrong; he's still guilty of murder in his heart.

Or consider this: You've promised to help your classmates collect canned goods for the poor. But when the time comes, you don't do it because you're sick at home with the flu. You don't follow through on your original good choice. But does this make you morally wrong?

No. You really would keep your promise if it were physically possible.

Freedom is your inner, spiritual ability to choose to be the kind of person you decide to be. Liberty is the external power you have—or don't have—to act out your choice. Freedom depends on truth and values. Liberty depends on power. True freedom directs us by God and toward God.

F.Y.I.

The Bill of Rights, which defines the basic liberties of U.S. citizens, was not part of the original constitution. It was added on as the first ten amendments. It then took almost another one hundred years to outlaw slavery.

50

Chapter 4 Quiz Answers (continued)

2. The first three commandments set up the ground rules for the respect we owe to God. Through these commandments, we have a moral obligation to praise and to trust God, to respect God, and to love and honor God as the center of our lives. And the laws of the Church take the general moral values found in the Ten Commandments and translate them into specific practices for Catholics to follow. Also, civil laws are oftentimes based on the Ten Commandments. The basic purpose of civil laws is to protect human rights.

3. Answers may vary.

Too many choices

Sometimes we have so many choices, we don't know which one to choose. Read the following story.

Carmen has just finished dinner. The rest of the evening is all planned. She simply has to study for a very important science test, her worst subject. Passing or failing for the year depends on doing well on tomorrow's test. Then it hits her: Tonight's the night for the big two-hour TV special that's been advertised all month. She really wants to watch it.

As Carmen is struggling to decide what to do, the phone rings. It's Kayla, her best friend. Kayla wants to know if Carmen can come over and study with her. Kayla also has a new CD they can listen to. Carmen knows if she goes to Kayla's house she'd never be able to study very well. But she doesn't want to turn Kayla down. So Carmen stalls, telling Kayla she'll call right back after she checks with her parents. Carmen hangs up and sits there, trying to decide what to do.

Just then her favorite aunt, Maria, stops by. Aunt Maria explains that she won't be able to make it next week to Carmen's birthday party. She wants to take Carmen down to the mall tonight so they can pick out Carmen's gift and then go out for ice cream.

Suddenly, Carmen's life is very complicated. She has too many choices!

In a small group, discuss each choice Carmen has and what the results of each might be. Write the group's answers here.

(4)

Carmen's choices	Possible results

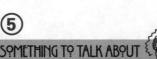

(5)

SOMETHING TO TALK ABOUT

1. What is the morally right choice for Carmen to make? Why?

2. Can you think of another situation in which a young person has too many options? What's the situation? What do you think is the morally right choice to make? Why?

3. Ask volunteers to take turns reading aloud **Too many choices**.

4. Have the students form small groups to complete the chart on page **51**.

5. As a class, discuss the two **Something to talk about** questions. Encourage everyone to say something.

Optional

Have the students take turns reading Genesis 3. This chapter helps answer the questions "Why do people suffer?" and "Why does evil exist?" Because the first humans chose to disobey God, God expelled them from Eden. Life outside the perfect friendship with God is hard; God did not abandon the first humans, but they and their descendants have suffered and had to work hard.

Resource Center

Chapter Overview

The chapter defines freedom as the capacity to make choices. This capacity distinguishes us from animals and, in a real sense, is what makes us human. Animals must follow their instincts and act according to their nature. We can either follow or contradict our conscience. Ultimately, we decide for ourselves the kind of person we end up being.

Catechism Background

For more information on freedom and responsibility, you may want to read the *Catechism of the Catholic Church* (#s 1731–48).

The Language of Faith

Free will is the God-given ability to choose between good and evil.

Materials

• Bibles (optional)

1. Ask volunteers to take turns reading aloud the section on page **52** entitled **Being human**. Discuss the text by asking these questions:

   - What are two ways that humans are different from animals?

   - Can animals be moral? Why?

   - What does the text mean when it says, "The more freedom we have, the more responsibility we also have"?

Optional

Have the students read Romans 7. In this chapter, Paul talks about the irony that all of us have experienced: Laws and rules like the Ten Commandments exist to guide us to do the right thing, but sometimes when we are told "Don't do this," we are tempted even more to do what is wrong. Paul's lengthy talk about our human weakness and sinfulness might be discouraging except for this: He reminds us that through Jesus Christ we have new life in the Spirit. What we find difficult to do on our own—follow God's will—we can do with the help of the Spirit.

Materials
   - Bibles (optional)

Being human

Do you know that only human beings have the freedom to choose right or wrong? This is because only humans have a conscience. We are free to follow our conscience or to go against it. Animals, instead, have instincts and appetites that make them behave in certain ways. For this reason, squirrels in the wild always do what squirrels are supposed to do. Likewise, bears do what bears are supposed to do. So do ducks, alligators, and rabbits.

In terms of morality, a squirrel or a monkey may seem to "have it made." But few people would really want to trade places with an animal. The good news about human freedom—the ability to choose—is that we aren't robots or puppets or animals that are totally controlled by natural instinct or by outside forces.

Even at your age, when parents and other adults still have a great deal of control over you and make many decisions for you, you already are beginning to have a real ownership of your life. You are your own person. You are in charge, or in control, of some decisions. The older you get, the more you'll be able to exercise ownership over yourself. When it comes to your life, you'll be in the driver's seat rather than "going along for the ride."

In addition to having the freedom to choose right or wrong, humans are the only creatures on the earth who can see beyond the present moment. To a certain extent, we can predict what the future results of our actions will be. For example, if you don't study for a test, you can predict that you'll probably get a poor grade. If you steal, you can expect that someone will feel wronged. And you can expect to be punished if you get caught.

Because of our ability to choose right or wrong and because of our ability to "see" the possible consequences of our actions, we are *responsible* for the decisions we make. In other words, the other side of freedom is responsibility. The more freedom we have, the more responsibility we also have. And the more we choose to do good, the freer we become by cooperating with God's grace.

All humans want freedom to choose for themselves. But not everybody wants to accept the responsibility that goes with it. If you want ownership of your own life, you have to accept responsibility for how you live that life. Whether Carmen in the story on page 51 passes science for the year is up to her. It depends on how she uses her freedom and the choice she makes. That's what being human—and adult—is all about.

52

Resource Center

Chapter Overview

The chapter distinguishes between freedom (the capacity to choose) and liberty (the power to act out one's choices). As the students will learn, people remain free even if they have no liberty. We remain responsible for our good and bad choices even if we don't always have the power or liberty to act out our choices.

Catechism Background

For further information on the morality of human acts, you may want to read the *Catechism of the Catholic Church* (#s 1749–61).

For further information on freedom and responsibility, you may want to read the *Catechism of the Catholic Church* (#s 1731–38).

Freedom and responsibility

Some of the parables Jesus told are about human freedom and responsibility. In a small group, read and summarize the following two parables. Then discuss how each item listed might represent a choice made today by young people in a moral situation.

Luke 8:4–15 Summary:
Jesus tells the parable of the sower who sows seed on different kinds of soil.

Item from parable	Modern moral situation	The choice made
Birds		
Rocky ground		
Thorns		
Good soil		

Luke 19:11–27 Summary:
Jesus tells the parable of three servants who did different things with the money their master entrusted to them.

Item from parable	Modern moral situation	The choice made
Servant who earned a big return		
Servant who earned a moderate return		
Servant who buried the coins		

If time permits, share the group's example with the class.

2. Distribute Bibles. Have the students form small groups to read the two Scripture passages and to complete the two charts in the **Freedom and responsibility** activity. If there is time, call on the groups to share their examples.

Chapter Overview

Freedom is directly tied to knowledge on the one hand and responsibility on the other. Lack of knowledge of our choices limits our freedom to choose and, therefore, removes responsibility to some degree or even entirely. Certain things can limit our knowledge and consequently can limit our freedom and responsibility. Age (immaturity) and mental defect can limit knowledge. Limited opportunities to learn can limit knowledge. Strong emotions, such as fear and anger, can temporarily impair our ability to make choices.

Materials
• Bibles

1. Allow time for the students to work alone to complete the two **Journal** entries on page **54**.

2. Ask volunteers to take turns reading aloud the text, **Freedom and immaturity**. Discuss as needed.

3. Ask another student to read aloud the **F.Y.I.** section, or allow time for the students to read this section on their own. Discuss as needed.

4. Draw the students' attention to the **Catechism Connection**. Make sure the students realize that ALL people, even those with mental handicaps and mental illnesses, have dignity and are loved by God.

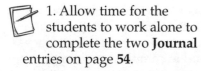

 1. This is how the parable of the sower may be seen in my life:
_____
_____

2. This is how the parable of the talents may be seen in my life:
_____
_____

Freedom and immaturity ②

Has your mom or dad ever told you a funny story about when you were a baby? Maybe you got into your mom's perfumes and smelled up the whole house before you were caught. Or maybe you climbed up on the table and got into the jar of jelly, making a total mess of yourself and the kitchen. Parents usually laugh when they tell stories of your mischief as a baby. So why they don't laugh now when your room is a mess, or when you experiment with smoking, or when you stay out later than they had agreed on?

The answer is easy enough. At your age, you're supposed to act in more mature ways. You're supposed to be able to think reasonably and to figure out that certain actions have certain consequences. Babies have not yet matured in their ability to think or to reason. As a result, they don't know the effects of their actions. They aren't really free to choose in a responsible way. Indeed, immaturity limits freedom, which in turn determines responsibility. A mathematician might write it this way: No maturity = no ability to choose = no responsibility.

The ability to reason usually starts at about age six or seven. That's when human freedom begins and when we start to become morally responsible. But seven-year-olds still aren't able to reason as well as someone your age. Your power to reason and to think through the results of your choices has reached an almost adult level. You have the needed maturity to know right from wrong. That gives you greater freedom to choose, and it gives you more responsibility for what you choose.

F.Y.I. ③

People with mental disabilities are limited in their ability to reason or to think clearly. People with problems that prevent them from being able to reason aren't actually free. We don't hold them responsible for what they do—at least not in the same way we would if they were healthy and whole.

Catechism Connection ④

The dignity of the human person implies and requires uprightness of moral conscience. . . . (1780)

Conscience enables one to assume responsibility for the acts performed. . . . (1781)

54

Resource Center

Scripture Background

Two versions of the Ten Commandments are found in the Bible. One appears in *Exodus 20:1–17* and the other in *Deuteronomy 5:6–21*. The story of the Ten Commandments was passed from generation to generation for hundreds of years. During that long period the story as well as the commandments took on two slightly different forms. Eventually both were written down as we have them today, and both inspired versions were considered part of the Bible.

⑤

Pretend that you are a lawyer. Sign up for one of the following cases. For each case, form two teams, one "pro" and one "con," to debate the case. Write down your arguments in the space provided. Then actually hold a debate about each case in class.

The case	The "pro" position	The "con" position
A 15-year-old boy kills another boy in a gang dispute. Should the boy be tried as an adult or as a juvenile?	The boy should be tried as an adult because:	The boy should be tried as a juvenile because:
A 14-year-old girl who is severely mentally challenged burns down her house when playing with a cigarette lighter. Her little brother is killed in the fire. Should the girl stand trial for a crime or should she be sent to a mental hospital?	The girl should stand trial because:	The girl should be sent to a mental hospital because:

⑥ *Class debate.*

⑦ On a scale of 1 to 10, with 1 being very immature and 10 being very mature, how do you rate yourself right now? Why?

_____

_____

Freedom and ignorance **⑧**

A second factor affects human freedom and responsibility. That factor is knowledge. It's important to know what the options are *before* you make a decision. That way you can freely choose between the different options. *Before* you act, it's also important to know that a certain action is right and that another action is wrong. That way you can be fully responsible for your choice.

Ignorance does limit our freedom and decrease our responsibility in matters of right and wrong. But for a mature person, ignorance is never an excuse for acting in a morally wrong way. We have a responsibility to have an informed conscience.

Consider this example: Suppose your cat is coughing and sneezing and looking miserable. You want to help, so you give the cat some of the cold medication your parents give you when you have a cold. To your surprise and horror, the cat

dies. You feel terrible because you know what you did killed the cat. Are you responsible? Yes, you are. But you're not as responsible as if you had deliberately poisoned the cat. After all, you honestly didn't know that aspirin could kill your pet. You didn't intend to do harm.

Now consider this situation: Your school has somebody come in to talk to your class about bicycle safety. You feel that this is kid stuff, so you choose to goof off during the talk. A month later, you use an incorrect hand signal because you don't know the correct signal. A car has to swerve to avoid hitting you and smashes into a parked car. Nobody is hurt, but there is a lot of damage. Are you responsible? You bet! You've *freely* chosen to remain ignorant. That makes you *responsible* for your ignorance and for any harm your *unnecessary ignorance* causes.

---

6. Hold a debate in class about each case. Perhaps select a panel of judges to decide which team has "won."

7. Allow time for the students to work alone to complete the **Journal** entry.

8. Ask volunteers to take turns reading aloud the text, **Freedom and ignorance**.

Teaching Tip

Clarifying concepts: Reassure the students that they cannot commit sins by mistake. They have to want to do something that they know is wrong and understand the choice they have made. We are responsible for learning to the best of our abilities how to make good choices. A person's responsibility for his or her actions may be lessened due to ignorance, fear, duress, or other psychological or social factors.

1. As a class, discuss the **Something to talk about** question on page **56**. Make sure the students realize that no one is perfect. No single person can know everything. What is important is that we remain open to learning and that we try to learn from our mistakes.

2. Ask volunteers to take turns reading aloud **Freedom and strong emotions**. Discuss as needed.

3. Ask another student to read aloud the **F.Y.I.** section, or allow time for the students to read this section on their own. Discuss as needed.

4. Allow time for the students to work alone to complete the two **Journal** entries.

5. Ask volunteers to take turns reading aloud **Types of sin**.

Optional

Divide the students into three groups. Assign each group one of the three factors that affect human freedom and responsibility: immaturity, ignorance, and strong emotion. Allow time for the groups to prepare a role-play of a situation that demonstrates how the factor assigned to them affects the responsibility to make daily choices.

① SOMETHING TO TALK ABOUT

What are some examples of ignorance on the part of junior high students that might limit freedom or reduce responsibility?

Freedom and strong emotions ②

Strong emotion is a third factor that affects human freedom and responsibility. Sometimes our emotions can be so strong that we can temporarily lose our freedom to choose. Great fear, for example, can mess up our thinking and our judgment. We can get so scared that we don't see all the choices. We only see the choice that will help us escape the danger we are in.

Consider this true example: A helicopter pilot loses his bearings and accidentally flies over enemy territory. He is shot down and captured. While he is in prison, government officials torture him and threaten to kill him if he does not sign a false confession against his country. Out of fear, the man signs the statement—both lying and committing an act of disloyalty against his country. What he's done is wrong, but he's not fully responsible. He was forced into this action. Great fear made him less free and less responsible.

The same thing can happen in daily life. For example, peer pressure can sometimes produce in young people great fear (fear of being laughed at, fear of being rejected by a group, fear of disappointing people who love and depend on you). Such fear can keep you from seeing things clearly and from responding freely. You can become so afraid that you end up doing things you'd never think of doing if you were alone.

This is tricky, of course. You can't use fear as a pat excuse for every wrong choice you make. Emotional fear can be very real, and it can limit freedom and responsibility. However, the more you believe in your human dignity, given by God, the more you will be able to resist peer pressure and the resulting fear.

Besides fear, other emotions can sometimes rob us of freedom, too. For example, some people "go crazy" with anger or rage or jealousy or despair. They can no longer think clearly, and they lose their ability to choose freely. So they commit a "crime of passion." They kill someone, or they do something violent to get revenge, or they try to commit suicide. Again, we have to be

careful not to use these emotions as an excuse to avoid responsibility. In God's plan for humans, we are to be in control of our emotions; they must not control us.

F.Y.I. ✎ ③

Over eighty percent of all murders in the United States are "crimes of passion."

④

On a scale of 1 to 10, with 1 being "emotions control my life" and 10 being "I'm always in control of my emotions," rate yourself right now. Why did you rate yourself the way you did? Give examples.

_____
_____
_____
_____
_____

What is one way I can gain better control over my emotions and thus be more free?

_____
_____

Types of sin ⑤

Whenever we do moral wrong, we commit a sin. We sin against ourselves or others or God. But how serious our sin is—how morally responsible we are for doing wrong—depends on several factors. That's one reason the Church defines some sins as *venial* and others sins as *mortal*.

In order for a sin to be mortally wrong, three conditions must exist. First, the action must be seriously wrong (for example, murder, kidnapping a child, burning down a building). Second, we must know *beforehand* that the action is seriously wrong. And third, we must freely and completely decide to act wrongly. If a wrong action does not have these three conditions, the sin is not mortal, but venial.

56

Resource Center

Catechism Background

For further information on freedom and strong emotions and passions, you may want to read the *Catechism of the Catholic Church* (#s 1735, 1762–70).

The students may have many questions about sin and evil. To help you guide their explorations on these topics, read the *Catechism of the Catholic Church* on evil, sin, and original sin (#s 385–409).

Scripture Background

Genesis 3:1–24 is allegory intended to teach us about our relationship with God and about the human tendency to sin. Allegorical stories use symbols to represent deeper truths. Thus the story's details—the tree of knowledge, the serpent, the fruit, and so forth—are not meant to be interpreted literally.

⑥ Catechism Connection

Sin is an offense against reason, truth, and right conscience. . . . (1849)

For a sin to be mortal, three conditions must together be met: "Mortal sin is sin whose object is grave matter and which is also committed with full knowledge and deliberate consent." (1857)

Scripture Search ⑦

Work in groups of three or four to complete this activity. Read each of the following Scripture passages. Then decide if the sin committed is mortal or venial. Give your reasons in the space provided. When you have finished, discuss your group's decisions with the class.

Scripture Passage	Mortal or venial sin?	Why?
Genesis 4:1–9 **Cain kills his brother Abel because he is jealous.**		
2 Samuel 11 **David has Uriah killed so that he can be with Uriah's wife, Bathsheba.**		
Matthew 26:69–75 **Out of fear, Peter denies knowing Jesus.**		

⑧ **Class discussion.**

57

 6. Draw the students' attention to the **Catechism Connection** on page 57. Make sure the students understand the difference between a mortal sin and a venial sin.

 7. Distribute Bibles. Have the students form groups of four or five to complete the **Scripture Search** activity.

8. As a class, discuss the groups' answers to the **Scripture Search**.

Optional

Review with the students the penitential rite of the Mass in which we acknowledge our sinfulness and ask God's forgiveness. We may pray the I Confess prayer (on page **98**); the Lord, Have Mercy; or another short prayer.

The Language of Faith

- *Sin* is a free and willful turning away from God's law and love. We are called to live in union with God and others. It is God who extends this invitation. To sin is to ignore God's invitation. We can sin through our thoughts, words, or deeds (commission) or by failing to do something we should do (omission). Sin can be serious (mortal) or less serious (venial).

- The word *venial* means "easily excused or forgiven." A venial sin is a "small" sin that weakens our relationship with God but does not destroy it. Nevertheless, followers of Jesus try hard to avoid all sin. Catholics who have committed venial sins are encouraged but not required to receive the Sacrament of Reconciliation frequently.

Catechism Background

For further information on mortal and venial sin, you may want to read the *Catechism of the Catholic Church* (#s 1854–64, 1874–76).

Materials
- Bibles

57

1. Ask volunteers to take turns reading aloud **Freedom and you** on page **58**.

 2. As a class, discuss the two **Something to talk about** questions.

3. Gather the students, with their books and a pen/pencil, in the designated prayer corner or sacred space. If fire laws permit, light a candle.

4. After the students have become settled, ask a volunteer to read 1 Peter 2:16–17 (page **58**). Invite the students to reflect silently on what they have heard.

5. After a brief period of silence, ask the students to discuss practical ways that young people can grow in freedom and moral responsibility.

6. Allow time for the students to complete the **Journal** entry.

7. Pray together the prayer.

Optional

Conclude the **Reflection** by listening to or by singing an appropriate song.

- "All That We Have" by Gary Ault from *Glory & Praise* (OCP [NALR]), *Gather (Comprehensive)* (GIA).

- "Song of Thanksgiving" by The Dameans from *Gather (Comprehensive)* (GIA).

- "We Are Called" by David Haas from *Gather (Comprehensive)* (GIA).

Freedom and you

It may sound as if moral responsibility is very complicated. It isn't. Basically, you have the God-given freedom to choose to be human or to choose to act in a less than human way. When you use your freedom to make wrong choices, you are responsible for the effects this has on you and on anyone else who is hurt in the process. When you freely make good choices, you are acting in a morally responsible way.

Most likely, you already have an adult capacity to reason and to think through the effects of most of your choices. This capacity makes you *free*. It also makes you *responsible*. You can still act like a child, but you can't really be a child again. It's too late. Even thought your parents and other adults still make many choices for you, most of these choices deal with externals (when you have to be home, how much money you get to spend, what parties you can go to, etc.). The real choices—choices that determine who you are—are up to you. For example, you must choose to be generous or selfish, truthful or a cheater, kind or a bully. Parents can't make those choices for you.

At this time in life, you are beginning to be in charge of your own life. *You* are responsible for who you are and what you do. You know what God expects of you. You understand the commandments and the law of love. These things help you make morally mature decisions. You can handle this adult responsibility to shape yourself and to be fully human, to become the person God created you to be. God thinks you can do this and has provided you with the power and the freedom to choose the good.

SOMETHING TO TALK ABOUT

1. Do you think God is giving us too much responsibility by expecting us to choose what we will ultimately become? Why or why not?

2. Can people your age handle the responsibility to be morally adult? Why or why not?

 Gather for prayer.

Reflection

 *As servants of God, live as free people, yet do not use your freedom as a pretext for evil. Honor everyone. Love the family of believers. Fear God. (1 Peter 2:16–17)*

Briefly discuss how young people today can grow in freedom and moral responsibility.

 Here is one way I will try this week to grow in freedom and moral responsibility:

_____

_____

_____

Jesus,

Help me be grateful for and appreciative of the freedom I have been given.

Help me increase my knowledge so that I can make good choices, and help me be responsible for the choices I make.

Help me not bend to peer pressure when I know what I am doing is right.

Amen.

58

Resource Center

Chapter Overview

Because junior high students have reached an almost adult capacity to reason and to know, they experience a basically adult freedom to choose. This chapter also shows them that they have a comparable adult responsibility for the choices they make even now.

Reference Sources

For help in addressing the students' questions about the unit's topics, see:

- *Whatever Happened to Sin?—The Truth about Catholic Morality* by Charles E. Bouchard OP (Liguori Publications, 1996).

HOMEWORK

Use a Bible to fill in the following blanks.

Isaiah 61:1 The _____ of the Lord GOD is upon me, because the LORD has

_____ me; he has sent me to bring _____ _____ to the

oppressed, to bind up the _____ , to proclaim _____ to

the captives, and release to the _____ . . . .

John 8:31–32 Then Jesus said to the Jews who had believed in him, "If you continue in my

_____ , you are truly my _____ ; and you will

_____ the truth, and the truth will make you _____ ."

Romans 8:2 For the law of the _____ of life in _____

_____ has set you free from the law of _____ and of

_____ .

Galatians 5:1 For _____ Christ has set us free. _____

_____ , therefore, and do not submit again to a yoke of _____ .

59

---

8. Remind the students to do the **Homework** and to review the chapter for the next class.

Optional

There will be a short quiz at the beginning of the next class.

Answers to the Homework

Depending on the version of the Bible used, the students' answers may not match exactly but should be synonyms of the words listed here.

Isaiah 61:1 The <u>Spirit</u> of the Lord GOD is upon me, because the LORD has <u>anointed</u> me; he has sent me to bring <u>good news</u> to the oppressed, to bind up the <u>brokenhearted</u>, to proclaim <u>liberty</u> to the captives, and release to the <u>prisoners</u>. . . .

John 8:31–32 Then Jesus said to the Jews who had believed in him, "If you continue in my <u>word</u>, you are truly my <u>disciples</u>; and you will <u>know</u> the truth, and the truth will make you <u>free</u>."

Romans 8:2 For the law of the <u>Spirit</u> of life in <u>Christ Jesus</u> has set you free from the law of <u>sin</u> and of <u>death</u>.

Galatians 5:1 For <u>freedom</u> Christ has set us free. <u>Stand firm</u>, therefore, and do not submit again to a yoke of <u>slavery</u>.

Multimedia Resources

Come and See, produced by ACTA Publications (video) (BROWN-ROA, 1-800-922-7696).

Stories of the Human Spirit, "The Smoker," produced by ACTA Publications (video) (BROWN-ROA, 1-800-922-7696).

5: Freedom to Choose
Review Quiz

True or False

_____ 1. All people, even those with mental handicaps or mental illnesses, have dignity.

_____ 2. Ignorance is always a good excuse for bad choices.

_____ 3. Liberty and freedom are the same thing.

_____ 4. The ability to reason usually starts at about age eleven or twelve.

_____ 5. Mental defects can limit a person's ability to know or to think clearly.

_____ 6. Being adult means being responsible for your choices.

Fill in the Blanks

1. The other side of freedom is _____.

2. The more you believe in human dignity, given by God, the more you will be able to resist peer pressure and the resulting _____.

3. Freedom is the capacity to _____.

4. _____ is the ability to carry out the choices you make.

5. Three conditions are necessary for a sin to be mortal: (1) The action must be _____. (2) You must know _____ that the action is seriously wrong. (3) You must freely and completely _____ to act wrongly.

6. The more we choose to do good, the freer we become by cooperating with _____ _____.

5: Freedom to Choose
Review Quiz

Essay

1. Discuss the difference between freedom and liberty and the effects that this difference has on moral choices.

2. Tell the ways in which responsibility, immaturity, ignorance, and strong emotions have an effect on freedom.

3. List some guidelines for using your freedom in a moral way as you mature and move through life.

BROWN-ROA, a division of Harcourt Brace & Company

6
Lesson Procedure

Academic Goals: To understand the nature and significance of the different kinds of moral decisions and to know the most effective ways of making these kinds of choices.

Attitudinal Goal: To appreciate the importance of everyday decisions in shaping us as moral persons.

1. Go over the chapter 5 **Homework** answers, found on page **59**.

2. Review chapter 5 by giving the students a quiz. Reproduce page **59A** and/or page **59B** and give one to each student. After the students have completed the quiz, collect them to correct later. If you wish, correct the quizzes in class with the students.

Optional

As the students take the review quiz, collect their textbooks and journals. Scan the pages to make sure the students are completing the **Journal** activities. Also scan for indications of problems that should be addressed.

3. Have the students read silently **Decisions you've made** and work alone to complete the chart on page **60**. Emphasize that these are NOT moral decisions (decisions between right and wrong) but rather ordinary decisions (decisions between two good choices). As a class, discuss the answers to the chart.

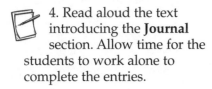 4. Read aloud the text introducing the **Journal** section. Allow time for the students to work alone to complete the entries.

---

① *Discuss homework assignment.* ② *Give students the review quiz.*

6 Making Decisions

Decisions you've made ③

If you're like most people, you've probably made hundreds, even thousands of decisions this past week. Many of these decisions had nothing to do with right or wrong. They were simply choices between two good options. Write down one decision you've made this week regarding each of the following categories. Then discuss your decisions in class.

Category	A decision I made between two good choices
Food	
Clothes	
Transportation	
Shoes	
Leisure time	
Homework	
TV	
Chores	

④

Other decisions you've made during the week probably dealt with a choice between right and wrong. Such decisions are called *moral decisions*.

1. One moral decision I made this week that was right:
_____
_____

2. What helped me make that right decision?
_____
_____
_____

60

Chapter 5 Quiz Answers

True or False

1. T	4. F
2. F	5. T
3. F	6. T

Fill in the Blanks

1. responsibility	4. Liberty
2. fear	5. seriously wrong, beforehand, decide/choose
3. choose	6. God's grace

Essay

1. Freedom is our inner, spiritual ability to choose to be the kind of person we decide to be, a power that can't be taken away from us without actually destroying who we are. Liberty is the external power we have to act out our choice. This ability can be taken away from us without destroying who we are. Being morally good depends on how we use our freedom, not our liberty. Morality depends on the choices we make with our freedom, whether or not we have the liberty to carry out those choices.

Moral decisions—three types ⑤

There are three types of moral decisions. The first is the "everyday" kind. It's a fairly ordinary decision you make on a typical day. The second type is the "snap" decision. You make this kind of decision on the spur of the moment, without thinking or planning ahead of time. The third kind of decision isn't so common, but it's very important. It's the "big" decision, because so much is at stake. Your whole life may change because of the choice you make.

Here's an example of each type of moral decision:

1. **Everyday decision.** You really want to see a new movie that's in town. It's rated R, and your parents have made it very clear that you can't go to R-rated movies. The movie is playing at the multi-theater cinema. There's a PG movie playing at the same time in another part of the cinema. You ask to go to the PG movie, which is okay with your parents. But all along, you know you'll go to the R movie once they drop you off.

2. **Snap decision.** You're hanging out with a group of friends at the park one evening. Not much is happening. Suddenly, one of your friends produces a couple of marijuana cigarettes. He says he found them in his older sister's room. He asks if anybody wants to try one. Your best friend is willing to see what it's like. Then a few more agree. Without much thinking, you say you'll try it, too.

3. **Big decision.** A friend admits to you in confidence that's he's been fooling around with cocaine. You've heard a lot about cocaine, but he's the first person you've ever met who has actually tried it. He doesn't ask you to try it. You wouldn't try it even if he did. But he does tell you the way he gets his cocaine. He does "errands" for a college kid who is a pusher. It's clear to you that your friend is getting into very deep water. You really like him and don't want him to mess up his life like this. You try to talk him out of using cocaine and working for the pusher. He just laughs. Now what do you do? Do you tell his parents or other authorities about it? Do you mind your own business? Do you stop being friends? None of the choices seems very appealing, but you have to choose one because so much is at stake.

SOMETHING TO TALK ABOUT ⑥

1. What are other examples of everyday moral decisions that young people might make?

2. What are other examples of snap moral decisions that young people might make?

3. What would you choose to do in the "big decision" example? Why?

4. What are other examples of big moral decisions that young people might make?

5. Ask volunteers to take turns reading aloud the section on page **61** entitled **Moral decisions—three types**.

6. As a class, discuss the four **Something to talk about** questions.

Optional

Invite the students to reflect on books they've read or on TV programs or movies they've seen that explore moral questions. Have each student write a one-page report on an episode from a favorite TV show or on a favorite book or movie. Have the students discuss the following questions in their report:

- What choices did the characters face?
- How did they come to their decisions?
- What were the results of their choices?
- Would you have chosen differently?
- What do you think Jesus would have told the characters to help them choose?

2. The more freedom we have, the more responsibility we have. And the more we choose to do good, the freer we become by cooperating with God's grace. Immaturity limits freedom, which in turn determines responsibility: No maturity = no ability to choose = no responsibility. Ignorance limits our freedom and decreases our responsibility in matters of right and wrong. It's important to know what the options are before you make a decision. It's also important to know that a certain action is right and that another action is wrong. And sometimes our emotions are so strong that we temporarily lose our freedom to choose.

3. Answers may vary.

1. Ask volunteers to take turns reading aloud **Everyday decisions** on page **62**. Discuss the text by asking these questions:

   • How can lying become a pattern?

   • Is it true that it becomes easier to do something that is wrong if it is repeated?

   • Can you think of any examples of adults you know who are living out patterns of behavior begun earlier in life? (No names, please.)

   • Can you give an example of a life direction that was made one day at a time?

   • What do everyday decisions have to do with morality?

 2. Ask another volunteer to read aloud the **F.Y.I.** section, or allow time for the students to read this section on their own. Discuss as needed.

3. Draw the students' attention to the **Catechism Connection**. Make sure the students understand that both sin (vice) and virtue are habits. We tend to make the same decisions (to do right or to do wrong) over and over again.

4. Have the students form groups of three or four. Allow time for them to complete the **Virtue or Vice?** activity on page **62**. If time permits, have the groups present their stories to the class. Focus first on the stories about virtue. Then listen to the stories about vice.

Everyday decisions ①

The biggest part of your moral life is made up of everyday decisions. You make such decisions all the time. They're pretty routine. They don't deal with big issues, and they don't create big waves. But they probably play the biggest part in determining the kind of person you are—and will be. Here's an example:

Lying to your parents once about what movie you are going to see doesn't make you a big-time liar, but it's a start! Such lies are considered *venial sins*. It makes the next lie easier. Lying becomes more routine. You don't notice it because each decision to lie is a "little" decision and doesn't create any big problems. It may take months; it may take years. But if you continue to ignore these little decisions, you'll wake up some day and discover that you've created a liar out of yourself. Lying is now part of your makeup. You're a person who can't be trusted.

The same truth applies to selfishness, to bullying, to laziness, to talking badly about others behind their backs. Nobody decides all at once to spend his or her life as a selfish person, a bully, a lazy slob, or a cruel gossip. But many people *become* selfish, abusive, lazy, or cruel—one step at a time, one decision at a time, one day at a time.

The point is this: Every decision you make that goes against your conscience will have bad effects, even if you don't see these bad effects right away. There's no real escape from that fact. You can't keep making wrong decisions in small matters without having your decisions eventually catch up to you. The kind of person you will be five, ten, or fifteen years in the future is being decided *now*.

A pattern of venial sins, or less serious acts against God and others, can weaken our ability to be good. As a result, a person may more easily choose to sin in a more serious, or mortal, way. Such a person then turns away from God completely.

F.Y.I. ✎ ②

Judas didn't make his decision to betray Jesus all at once. He arrived at it slowly over several years, through the day-to-day decisions he was making while traveling with Jesus.

Catechism Connection ③

Sin creates a proclivity to sin; it engenders vice by repetition of the same acts. . . . (1865)

A virtue is a habitual and firm disposition to do the good. . . . (1803)

④  **Virtue or Vice?**

Work with two or three others. Write a story about a boy or girl your age whose everyday good decisions turn into a lifelong virtue (the habit of doing right). Then write a story about a boy or girl your age whose everyday bad decisions turn into a lifelong vice (the habit of doing wrong). Write down the group's stories here. If time permits, share the stories with the class.

Story 1: An everyday good decision that leads to lifelong virtue:
Title: _____
_____
_____
_____

Story 2: An everyday bad decision that leads to lifelong vice:
Title: _____
_____
_____
_____
_____

62

Resource Center

Chapter Overview

Typically we face three kinds of moral decisions—everyday decisions, snap decisions, and big decisions. Everyday decisions play a major role in shaping us because it is through these decisions that we develop our patterns of moral behavior. We don't become either saints or sinners all at once. We do this gradually, one decision at a time and one day at a time. Hence it is important to be alert to the *patterns* we are developing through our everyday decisions.

Teaching Tip

Clarifying concepts: To help students become more mature in their moral decision making, point out that the reward Jesus promises us for following the Beatitudes is not restricted to heaven in the future. Living the Beatitudes gives us and others real happiness now.

⑤

SOMETHING TO TALK ABOUT

1. Have you ever had an annoying habit, such as biting your nails or saying the same word over and over? Was it easy or hard to stop this habit? Why?

2. Many criminals who get out of jail become "repeat" offenders. They commit the same crime again. Why do you think this happens? Is it really possible for a criminal to change?

⑥

In terms of morality, this is who I want to be ten years from now:

_____
_____

Here's one way I will start today to become the future me:

_____
_____
_____

Snap decisions ⑦

It's often the snap decisions that get us in the most trouble. That's when we do the dumbest things and cause a great deal of harm to ourselves and others.

Just think about it: Whenever you've gotten yourself in the most trouble, wasn't it because of a snap decision? You went along with the gang. You acted on impulse. You didn't bother to think before you acted. Snap decisions seldom make you a permanently bad person, because they aren't the real "you" acting. But keep in mind that going along with the gang, acting on impulse, and not bothering to think aren't excuses. You are responsible for the bad effects of snap decisions. Such decisions often cause permanently bad results that you have to face the rest of your life. Each of us is required to have an informed conscience.

So how can you learn to deal with impulses and to make better decisions? Here are two tips:

1. Learn to anticipate. Most snap decisions are made in certain, predictable situations, such as when you're hanging out with a group and have no specific plans. Snap decisions are made when you're with certain people, when you're angry or psyched up.

63

---

5. As a class, discuss the two **Something to talk about** questions on page **63**.

6. Allow time for the students to work alone to complete the two **Journal** entries.

7. Ask volunteers to take turns reading aloud the text, **Snap decisions**. Discuss as needed.

Optional

To help the students apply the moral principles they are learning in class, have them role-play various situations calling for moral choices. Suggest situations involving moral dilemmas (or have the students suggest them) and ask volunteers to act out the resolution. Encourage the students to role-play the three different types of decisions: everyday decisions, snap decisions, and big decisions. Evaluate the results together as a class.

Chapter Overview

Snap decisions are often the most harmful. We make them on impulse, without thinking about consequences. In this chapter, students learn how to guard against snap decisions by learning to anticipate situations when they are most likely to be impulsive and do something foolish. Students also learn the importance of stopping and thinking through the consequences before making a decision.

Teaching Tip

Clarifying concepts: In discussing how to make good decisions, try not to give the impression that decisions are easy to make or difficult to change. Emphasize that whenever we make a decision that is contrary to our best interest, the Holy Spirit works to bring us back to the right path. Point out that we must be open to recognizing and seeking God's help. When we make a wrong decision that leads to sin, we can ask forgiveness and try to make things right.

1. Ask another volunteer to read the **F.Y.I.** section, or allow time for the students to read this section on their own. Discuss as needed.

2. Have the students form groups of four. Allow time for the groups to complete the first three sections of the **Smart strategies** activity on page **64**. Discuss the groups' answers.

3. As a class, decide on five things someone should think about before making a decision. Then discuss ways to help other young people avoid snap decisions.

 4. Allow time for the students to work alone to complete the two **Journal** entries.

Optional

Remind the students of the importance of prayer and reflection in making moral decisions and of examining their consciences periodically. Include time for such reflection in your classroom prayer on a regular basis. Suggest that the students visualize themselves in a favorite place, talking with Jesus. What choice would he want them to make? Remind the students that they can perform this kind of meditation anytime they are faced with a moral choice.

Learning to anticipate these predictable situations means getting to know yourself. Recall the times you most often made snap decisions that you regretted afterwards. (You wasted a lot of money; you went along with the group and did something wrong.) Try to learn from these past mistakes. Avoid these situations when you can. And when you can't avoid them, stay alert when you are in them. Be a little more cautious than usual.

2. Stop and take time to think. This isn't always easy, but it's almost always possible. Once you stop and think about your choice, it isn't a snap decision anymore. Chances are, it won't be a stupid decision, either. It's easy to see after the fact how dumb most snap decisions are. They'd look just as dumb before the fact, if you took time to think.

F.Y.I. ✏ ①

Unfortunately, some snap decisions have permanent consequences. Lives can be lost or ruined. Millions of dollars can be wasted. Kids your age can become unwed parents. The use of drugs, including alcohol, can become addictive.

②  **Smart strategies**

Form a group with three other classmates. Make a list of possible situations that might lead young people to make a snap decision. Write your list here:

Possible Situations

Brainstorm ways that young people can *anticipate* these situations before they actually happen. What are five things someone should think about before making a decision?

1. _____
2. _____
3. _____
4. _____
5. _____

Discuss your group's answers with the entire class. Then, as a class, agree on five things someone should think about before making a decision. Write the class's ideas here:

1. _____
2. _____
3. _____
4. _____
5. _____

As a class, discuss ways you can help other young people avoid snap decisions. ③

 Have you ever made a snap decision that you regretted? If it's not too personal, tell about it.
_____

What do you wish you would have done instead?
_____
_____

Resource Center

Teaching Tip

Clarifying concepts: To help the students make good moral choices, frequently review with them the steps in decision making. (1) Think about the choice before you act. (2) Ask yourself: "What is the right thing to do?" (3) Think about the results of your choice. (4) Ask yourself how Jesus would choose. (5) Compare your choice with the Great Commandment, the Ten Commandments, and the Beatitudes. (6) Talk about your choice with someone who can give you good advice. (7) Pray to the Holy Spirit for help.

Big decisions

Big decisions are the kind that can change your whole life, someone else's life, or both. Some big decisions might include whether or not to take drugs, which high school to attend, whether or not to go to college, what career to pursue, and whom to marry.

Luckily, at your age you don't have to deal with very many big decisions. But you will eventually face them—maybe even sooner than you'd like.

There are several things to do when facing big decisions. First, don't make any big decisions without praying. God knows you and loves you more than anyone. Go directly to God for advice. Lay out the problem, ask for help, and then listen. You aren't going to hear voices and you won't see answers flashed before your eyes, but things will become clearer. You've already received good direction through the Ten Commandments, the law of love, the Beatitudes, the Golden Rule, and the teachings of the Church. The Church assists us in forming a good conscience and making a good decision.

Second, don't make big decisions in a hurry. Have enough sense to get good advice.

In most big decisions you may face now, your best advisors will be among your parents, teach-ers, coaches, and adult relatives. Your pastor or other parish ministers can help shed some spiritual light on your decisions.

Good advisors will help you check out all the options you have. They'll help you think through the possible consequences of your decision. They'll share their own experiences with you. But how do you know who might be a good advisor?

Many young people turn to friends and classmates when they are trying to make an important decision. But this is not necessarily a good idea. Friends and classmates may like you and want you to be happy, but they usually don't have any more experience or expertise than you have. Likewise, advice columns found in daily newspapers and magazines may offer some good advice on occasion, but they aren't really written with you in mind and the writers seldom qualify as experts in things they write about.

These are the qualities of good advisors:
- Someone who knows you, loves you, and wants you to be happy.
- Someone who has the experience and expertise you don't have.
- Someone you feel safe with and who really knows how to listen.

5. Ask volunteers to take turns reading aloud the text on page **65**, **Big decisions**. Discuss as needed.

Optional

Remind the students that if we are open, the Holy Spirit will always help us pray. Invite them to compose a prayer asking the Holy Spirit to help them be open to grace and allow God to be the center of their lives, helping them make good decisions. Encourage the students to take these prayers home and share them with their families.

Optional

Have the students imagine that they have a big decision to make. Instruct them to write a short paragraph explaining the decision and their options. Have them formulate a list of questions they might ask their advisor.

Chapter Overview

Big decisions, which are rare, are very important because they change one's life direction in a major way. Whenever we face a big, life-changing decision, it is important to pray and to seek good advisors who are experienced and who care for us.

Link to the Faith Community

Point out that there are many resources in the faith community we can turn to for guidance. These include the parish staff and other parishioners. Ask the students to check the parish bulletin for the names of people they might consult when they need good advice.

Teaching Tip

Clarifying concepts: Explain that being wise does not necessarily mean being well-educated. Being wise has more to do with observing human nature, learning from experience, having common sense, and making good judgments.

1. Ask a volunteer to read the **F.Y.I.** section on page **66**, or allow time for the students to read this section on their own. Discuss as needed.

 2. Distribute Bibles. Allow time for the students to work alone to complete the **Scripture Search**. As a class, discuss the students' responses to the **Scripture Search** questions.

 3. Allow time for the students to work alone to complete the **Journal** entries.

Optional

Have the students read *Romans 6:4*. This passage supports the theme of the entire Letter to the Romans. God offers us redemption through the death and resurrection of Jesus. Baptism breaks the hold sin has over us, freeing us to live as Christ did—without sin. As Christians we have a moral duty to choose virtue and to avoid sin.

Materials

- Bibles

---

① F.Y.I.

Most people make less than ten major decisions during their entire life.

Scripture Search ② ✏️

Read each of the following Scripture passages. Summarize the passage. Then answer the questions.

1 Samuel 3 Summary:
Young Samuel seeks advice from the priest Eli and from God in prayer.

What "big decision" was facing Samuel?
He was trying to decide his vocation or career.

To whom did Samuel go for advice?
He went to Eli, the priest.

What advice was given?
To listen to God's voice.

What happened as a result of Samuel's decision?
Samuel became a respected prophet.

Matthew 1:18–25 Summary:
Joseph prays before deciding whether or not to marry Mary.

What "big decision" was facing Joseph?
He was trying to decide to marry Mary or to break off their engagement.

Who gave Joseph advice?
The Lord, in a dream, gave him advice.

What advice was given?
To marry Mary.

What happened as a result of Joseph's decision?
Jesus, the Savior, grew up in a loving family, with Joseph as his foster father.

③ What was the biggest decision you've ever had to make?
_____

To whom did you turn for advice? _____
Was this person a good advisor? _____ Why?
_____
_____

66

Resource Center

The Language of Faith

Prayer is the act by which we speak with and listen to God. Prayer can be vocal, consisting of words that are spoken, sung, or recited, as in the Lord's Prayer, or it can be mental, an act of opening oneself to God's presence through a technique such as meditation. Prayer is initiated by God, who moves us by grace to respond.

Teaching Tip

Clarifying concepts: When you find accounts of positive moral actions in the news media, share the information with the students. Together find out more about real-life people who are acting on values consistent with the Church's teaching. Students' role models often come only from among entertainment and sports figures. Help them look to a wider range of witnesses.

Four signs of a good decision

Every truly good moral decision has four distinguishing signs. First, the decision is prudent. That is, it is a very reasonable thing to do. Second, the decision is just. The decision is "fair" to you, to others, and to God. Third, the decision is lasting. If it's a good decision today, it'll also be a good decision tomorrow. The decision is truly worthwhile; you find strength to carry it out. Fourth, the decision is moderate. It lies in the middle between the two extremes of any kind of behavior.

The Church calls these four signs—prudence, justice, fortitude, temperance—the *cardinal virtues.* Like all virtues, they are habits that grow stronger the more we use them. The *Catechism of the Catholic Church* explains these virtues in the following way:

- Prudence disposes the practical reason to discern, in every circumstance, our true good and to choose the right means for achieving it. (1835)
- Justice consists in the firm and constant will to give God and neighbor their due. (1836)
- Fortitude ensures firmness in difficulties and constancy in the pursuit of the good. (1837)
- Temperance . . . provides balance in the use of created goods. (1838)

These four signs become a part of your life whenever you make a good moral decision. The more good decisions you make, the easier it is for you to be good and to do whatever is right. The reason for this is because these four virtues will become habits. With God's grace, they will become an essential part of who you are.

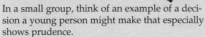

"In medio stat virtus" is an ancient idea of morality. It means "virtue lies in the middle." Another way to say it is "seek moderation in all things." Actually, it's a good rule in most cases.

SOMETHING TO TALK ABOUT

In a small group, think of an example of a decision a young person might make that especially shows prudence.

_____
_____
_____

What is a decision a young person might make that especially shows justice?

_____
_____

What is a decision a young person might make that especially shows fortitude?

_____
_____

What is a decision a young person might make that especially shows temperance?

_____
_____

67

---

4. Ask volunteers to take turns reading aloud **Four signs of a good decision**. Make sure the students understand the meaning of *prudence, justice, fortitude,* and *temperance.*

5. Ask another volunteer to read the **F.Y.I.** section, or allow time for the students to read this section on their own. Discuss as needed.

6. Have the students form small groups to discuss the **Something to talk about** questions. Or you may wish to conduct this discussion with the entire class.

Optional

Work with the class to brainstorm a list of people whose careers involve issues of justice. Examples include judge, attorney, social worker, police officer, elected official, missionary, union organizer, and human-rights activist. Invite family members who work in these professions to speak to the class about how they fight injustice.

The Language of Faith

Virtue, which comes from a Latin word meaning "strength," is a habitual and firm disposition to do good. It helps us grow in love of God and others. The theological virtues (faith, hope, and charity) are gifts from God and the foundation of Christian moral activity. They affect all our relationships. The moral virtues (prudence, justice, fortitude, and temperance) are acquired by human effort and help us live a morally good life.

Teaching Tip

Theological Virtues, Cardinal Virtues: According to Thomas Aquinas, virtues are habits—not in the sense of repeated, unthinking activities but understood as a combination of reason, will, and action oriented toward the good. The four *cardinal,* or "hinge," *virtues* are necessary to live a good human life. The *theological virtues*—God's free gifts—give us the ability to move toward unity with God.

1. Gather the students, with their books and a pen/pencil, in the designated prayer corner or sacred space. If fire laws permit, light a candle.

2. After the students have become settled, ask a volunteer to read Proverbs 4:7–8 (page **68**). Invite the students to reflect silently on what they have heard.

3. After a brief period of silence, ask the students to discuss people they know who are wise. Ask them to explain why they feel this way.

 4. Allow time for the students to complete the **Journal** entry.

5. Pray together the prayer.

Optional

Conclude the **Reflection** by listening to or by singing an appropriate song.

- "Blest Be the Lord" by Dan Schutte from *Glory & Praise* (OCP [NALR]), *Gather (Comprehensive)* (GIA), *Today's Missal* (OCP).

- "Lay Your Hands Gently Upon Us" by Carey Landry from *Glory & Praise* (OCP [NALR]).

- "The Cry of the Poor" by John Foley from *Today's Missal* (OCP).

- "You Are Near" by Dan Schutte from *Gather (Comprehensive)* (GIA), *Today's Missal* (OCP), *Glory & Praise* (OCP [NALR]).

- "Walking by Faith" by David Haas from *Walking by Faith* (BROWN-ROA, GIA).

---

(1) *Gather for prayer.*

Reflection

(2) *The beginning of wisdom is this: Get wisdom, and whatever else you get, get insight. Prize her highly, and she will exalt you; she will honor you if you embrace her. (Proverbs 4:7–8)*

Briefly discuss people you know who are wise. Explain why you feel this way. **(3)**

One way I will try this week to grow in wisdom and to make better decisions:
_____
_____

(5) *Jesus,*
Help me everyday to develop the habit of making good moral decisions.
Help me take time out to think and to pray for wisdom so that I avoid snap decisions.
Help me, when I must make important decisions, to seek help from good advisors.
Amen.

68

Resource Center

Chapter Overview

Learning to make good moral decisions takes practice, but like all habits, becomes easier the more we do it.

The Language of Faith

Grace is God's gift that enables us to share in the loving relationship that makes up the Holy Trinity. We do not earn grace; God gives it to us freely. In their definition of grace, theologians have included both our yearning for God and God's gift of himself.

HOMEWORK ⑥

Use this puzzle to complete the following paragraph.

1.   _ _ _ D
2.   _ _ E _ _ _ _ _
3. _ _ _ _ _ _ C _
4.   _ I _ _ _ _
5.   _ _ S _ _ _ _
6.   _ I _ _
7.   _ _ _ _ _ O _
8.   _ N _ _
9.   _ _ M _ _ _ _ _ _
10.   _ _ A _
11.   _ _ _ _ K
12.   _ _ _ _ I _ _ _ _
13.   _ N _ _ _ _ _ _ _ _
14.   _ _ G

The (1) of person you become in the future depends on (10) decisions you make now. To prevent yourself from making a (8) decision, you should learn to (13) and to take time to (11). (4) is the habit of making good (2) decisions and doing right. (6) is the habit of making bad decisions and doing wrong. When you have to make a (14) decision, you should get the help of a good (7). (3), (5), (9), and (12) are the cardinal virtues, four signs of a good decision.

69

---

6. Remind the students to do the **Homework** and to review the chapter for the next class.

Optional

There will be a short quiz at the beginning of the next class.

Answers to the Homework

1. kind	8. snap
2. everyday	9. temperance
3. Prudence	10. moral
4. Virtue	11. think
5. justice	12. fortitude
6. Vice	13. anticipate
7. advisor	14. big

Multimedia Resources

The Betrayal (video) (BROWN-ROA, 1-800-922-7696).

Stories of the Human Spirit, "The Smoker," produced by ACTA Publications (video) (BROWN-ROA, 1-800-922-7696).

Name: _____ Date: _____

6: Making Decisions
Review Quiz

True or False

_____ 1. A pattern of venial sins or less serious acts against God and others can weaken our ability to be good.

_____ 2. Snap decisions are usually minor and cause very little real harm.

_____ 3. Good advisors are people who know you, love you, and want you to be happy.

_____ 4. When facing a big decision, go directly to God for advice.

_____ 5. All decisions you make are moral decisions; they involve a choice between right and wrong.

_____ 6. Both sin (vice) and virtue are habits. People tend to repeat them.

Fill in the Blanks

1. The biggest part of your moral life is made up of _____ decisions.

2. To avoid snap decisions, it is important to take time to_____.

3. Good advisors have the _____ and expertise you don't have.

4. In forming a good conscience and making a good decision, we have the assistance of the

   _____.

5. Most good decisions have four distinguishing signs: _____, _____, _____,
   and _____.

6. In making moral decisions, it is important to _____ , to go to God for advice.

BROWN-ROA, a division of Harcourt Brace & Company

6: Making Decisions
Review Quiz

Essay

1. Discuss the long-range effects of everyday moral decisions.

2. Define the cardinal virtues and the effect they have on making a good decision.

3. What would be some essential rules to use in planning for a lifetime of good decision-making?

BROWN-ROA, a division of Harcourt Brace & Company

7

Lesson Procedure

Academic Goals: To understand more fully how faith transforms both freedom and responsibility and to see how the saints were people who made choices based on their faith and prophets helped others fight injustice.

Attitudinal Goal: To appreciate the fact that faith perfects human dignity rather than simply adding new "rules" to follow.

1. Go over the chapter 6 **Homework** answers, found on page **69**.

2. Review chapter 6 by giving the students a quiz. Reproduce page **69A** and/or page **69B** and give one to each student. After the students have completed the quiz, collect them to correct later. If you wish, correct the quizzes in class with the students.

Optional

As the students take the review quiz, collect their textbooks and journals. Scan the pages to make sure the students are completing the **Journal** activities. Also scan for indications of problems that should be addressed.

3. Have the students work alone to complete the **Eye puzzles** on page 70. As a class, discuss the answers to the activity.

   • Figure 1: Students will either see a vase or two people facing each other.
   • Figure 2: The lines are equal in length.
   • Figure 3: Students will either see a beautiful young woman or an elderly woman.
   • Figure 4: The boxes are equal.

 4. As a class, discuss the two **Something to talk about** questions.

70

---

 ① *Discuss homework assignment.* ② *Give students the review quiz.*

What Do You See?

③ Eye puzzles

Look at the figures on this page and answer the questions.

Figure 1
What do you see?

_____

Figure 3
What do you see?

_____

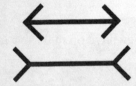

Figure 2
Which line is longer?

_____

Figure 4
Which box is larger?

_____

 ④ SOMETHING TO TALK ABOUT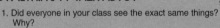
1. Did everyone in your class see the exact same things? Why?
2. Was it easy or hard to see a figure differently? Why?

70

Chapter 6 Quiz Answers

True or False

1. T 4. T
2. F 5. F
3. T 6. T

Fill in the Blanks

1. everyday
2. think
3. experience
4. Church
5. prudence, justice, fortitude, temperance (any order)
6. pray

Essay

1. The kind of person someone will be in the future is being decided now. A person can't keep making wrong decisions in small matters without having these decisions eventually catch up to him or her. A pattern of venial sins can weaken our ability to do good. As a result, a person may more easily choose to sin in a more serious way. Such a person then turns away from God completely.

Eyes of the beholder ⑤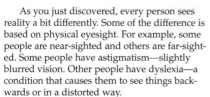

As you just discovered, every person sees reality a bit differently. Some of the difference is based on physical eyesight. For example, some people are near-sighted and others are far-sighted. Some people have astigmatism—slightly blurred vision. Other people have dyslexia—a condition that causes them to see things backwards or in a distorted way.

A second reason people see reality a bit differently is based on psychological eyesight—what people *expect* to see. For example, if you expect one box to be bigger than another box, then that's what you'll tend to see. It'll be very difficult for you to see the boxes another way.

There is also a third reason people see reality a bit differently. That reason has to do with spiritual eyesight. Spiritual eyesight means seeing beyond what is actually there and also seeing the *value* that is there.

We can begin to explain spiritual eyesight with the old saying, "Beauty is in the eyes of the beholder." What one person finds beautiful may

be the very same thing that someone else considers to be ugly. For example, suppose you have an old sled that you value more than anything because it belonged to your grandfather and then to your father and now is yours. Your friends think the sled is the weirdest piece of junk they've ever seen. But you don't agree. The sled is beautiful to you because of the way you see it. The sled isn't just a sled; it represents three generations of your family.

The same is true with faith. As you learned in an earlier chapter, faith gives us new eyes. Faith helps us see and value reality as God sees and values it. Because of faith, you can see yourself as a unique, special, precious child of God, even if you seem ordinary to everyone else. Moreover, when you see others through the eyes of faith, you realize that each person is just as unique and just as special as you are. The old lady across the street is special. The nameless baby dying of starvation in Africa is special. The kid whom everyone calls a "nerd" is special.

⑥ Class discussion.

71

5. Ask volunteers to take turns reading aloud the section on page **71** entitled **Eyes of the beholder**.

6. Ask the students for examples of things they or their parents value that others might consider worthless. Ask why they value these things. Perhaps start the conversation by sharing an example from your own life.

Optional

The early Christians sold their possessions to enter a community where spiritual goods were more important than material ones. In our world today we are surrounded by many opportunities to acquire possessions. This makes it difficult to demonstrate that spiritual goods are more important in our lives than material goods. Discuss with the students how Christians today can demonstrate that spiritual goods are a priority in their lives. (Possible answers: by charitable acts, time spent in prayer and celebrating the sacraments, limiting our possessions.)

2. The four cardinal virtues are prudence, justice, fortitude, and temperance. These four virtues become a part of our lives whenever we make a good moral decision. The more good decisions we make, the easier it is for us to be good and to do whatever is right. The reason for this is because these four virtues will become habits. With God's grace, they will become an essential part of who we are.

3. Answers may vary.

1. Divide the class into groups of four and distribute Bibles to each group. Allow time for the groups to complete the **What Jesus saw** activity on page **72**. If time permits, have each group share its "modern" Scripture story.

Optional

Have the students read *Matthew 9:36*. This verse follows passages describing a series of miracles in which Jesus reached out to various outcasts in society—a leper, a centurion, an elderly woman, people possessed by demons, a paralytic, a tax collector, two blind men, and a possessed mute. Like a good shepherd who loves and cares for each sheep in the flock, Jesus loves and cares for all people. Ask the students: In what ways was Jesus a shepherd to the crowds?

Materials
• Bibles

---

①  **What Jesus saw**

Jesus saw reality through the eyes of faith. He valued people and things as God values them. To help you understand the difference faith can make, form a group with three others. Read each of the following Scripture passages. Discuss what other people saw in each situation. Discuss what Jesus saw. Then discuss how "seeing with faith" affected the way Jesus acted.

Scripture	What others saw	What Jesus saw	How Jesus acted
Matthew 12:1–8 *Jesus defends his disciples who break the law to pick grain on the Sabbath.*			
Matthew 15:21–28 *Jesus cures the daughter of a Canaanite woman.*			
Mark 10:13–16 *Jesus welcomes little children.*			
Luke 7:36–50 *Jesus forgives the sins of a woman who is kind to him.*			
John 8:1–11 *Jesus deals mercifully with a woman everyone else has condemned.*			

As a group, rewrite one of the Scripture passages listed above in modern terms. Instead of having Jesus in the situation, write about a young person who "sees with faith." Write your story here. Then share it with the class.

_____

_____

_____

_____

_____

72

Resource Center

The Language of Faith

Faith is the gift given to us by God that moves us to seek him out and believe in him. Faith, hope, and love are the three *theological*, or God-given, virtues.

Link to Justice

Help the students see that in every aspect of our lives, we need to be aware of others' needs. Share with them the story of the Franciscan Missionaries of Jesus Crucified, founded in 1987. It is a group of lay people who live consecrated lives; they take vows and live a life of prayer. Anyone is welcome, but the group was founded especially for those who might not otherwise be admitted to a religious order because of their disabilities. Their patron is Blessed Kateri Tekakwitha, who was disfigured and partially blinded by smallpox and thereafter led a consecrated life as a layperson.

The extra mile

Being a follower of Jesus means imitating Jesus. It means "putting on his mind and heart," seeing reality with the eyes of faith. But being a true Christian means even more than this. It also means acting in ways that are consistent with our new way of seeing. It means going beyond what's right in an ordinary sense. It means doing *more*, going "the extra mile" beyond what we ordinarily would do.

Remember the formula: Knowledge = Freedom = Responsibility. If we add faith, the formula looks like this: Faith Knowledge = Christ-like Freedom = Christ-like Responsibility. Once we see things the way Christ does, we reach a new level of moral responsibility. We are expected to do more, to live out our faith in charity, which is expressed in the New Law, the law of love, grace, and freedom.

Catechism Connection

He who believes in Christ becomes a son of God. This filial adoption transforms him by giving him the ability to follow the example of Christ. It makes him capable of acting rightly and doing good. . . . (1709)

Living the extra mile

Jean Donovan was born on April 10, 1953, in Westport, Connecticut. Jean was involved in many sports, including softball, basketball, swimming, bike-riding, and horseback-riding. She graduated from college in 1975 with degrees in economics and political science. After receiving her master's degree in business management and accounting, Jean worked in Cleveland for a few years. Upon hearing about Cleveland's diocesan mission in El Salvador, she joined the Maryknoll Lay Missionary Program in Ossining, New York. She arrived in El Salvador in 1980 and worked with some of the sisters who were already there. She did bookkeeping, took care of nutritional needs, and led a youth choir. She taught the young people about the beauty of their bodies, minds, and souls. Most especially, they learned from Jean how much God loved them. She loved the children as Jesus did, and they loved her. On December 2, 1980, she and another sister drove to the airport to meet two Maryknoll sisters. After they had left the airport in their Jeep, Jean and the three missionary sisters were brutally murdered.

Scripture Search

To understand what "going the extra mile" means, read each of the following Scripture passages and summarize them here.

Matthew 5:38–42
Jesus gives examples of how we can go "the extra mile" for others.

Matthew 5:43–48
Jesus challenges us to love our enemies in addition to loving our friends and family members.

Matthew 18:21–22
We are not to count the times we forgive others.

Mark 10:17–31
Jesus tells a rich man that he should give all he has to the poor.

73

2. Ask volunteers to take turns reading aloud **The extra mile** on page **73**. Discuss as needed.

3. Draw the students' attention to the **Catechism Connection**. Remind the students that our choices to do right or wrong are linked to our identity, who we are. Because we believe that we are children of God, we have a moral obligation to act like children of God.

4. Ask volunteers to read **Living the extra mile**. Discuss as needed. Ask these questions:

- How did Jean act to lessen the effects of injustice? (*She fed the hungry.*)
- How did Jean act to lessen the causes of injustice? (*She taught young people that they had dignity.*)

5. Distribute Bibles. Have the students work either alone or in pairs to complete the **Scripture Search** activity. If time permits, have a class discussion about the meaning of the Scripture passages.

Chapter Overview

Faith heightens our awareness. It helps us see and value reality as God sees and values it. We can learn more about this heightened awareness by looking at the way Jesus treated others—the children no one wanted around, the sinful woman whom everyone condemned, the disciples who broke the law, foreigners, and so forth.

Teaching Tip

Students learn by example more easily than they learn from textbooks. So you yourself should be an example of how to live a Christian life. No one is perfect, but keep in mind that your actions and the way you treat others will be remembered longer than your words. Remember the respect with which Jesus, the greatest catechist and teacher, treated each of his listeners, and the way in which he invited them to choose the path of God's kingdom. You are called to touch each student's life in the same way.

Materials
- Bibles

1. As a class, discuss **The Right Thing** activity on page **74**. Allow time for the students to write down their answers. Encourage as many as possible to participate.

Optional

Have the students form small groups. Instruct the groups to prepare a role-play of a situation that shows a person going the extra mile and "putting on the mind and heart of Christ."

---

① **The Right Thing**

1. Suppose there is a new student in your class. Your group of friends wants nothing to do with him because he has a strange haircut and wears weird clothes. So your group ignores him and laughs at him behind his back.
   - What is the "ordinary" right thing to do?
   _____
   _____
   - What is the "going the extra mile" right thing to do?
   _____
   _____

2. Your younger sister gets into your room while you're not home. She listens to your CDs and doesn't put them back in the correct cases. You really get mad when you discover that your favorite CD is scratched.
   - What is the "ordinary" right thing for you to do?
   _____
   _____
   - What is the "going the extra mile" right thing to do?
   _____
   _____

3. Your class is having a food drive to help a family that has been left homeless due to a tornado. Each student has been asked to bring $5 worth of canned goods.
   - What is the "ordinary" right thing for you to do?
   _____
   _____
   - What is the "going the extra mile" right thing to do?
   _____
   _____

4. The elderly neighbor next door recently had a heart attack. He's pretty much confined to bed and can't go to the store for groceries, mow the lawn, or put out the trash on garbage day.
   - What is the "ordinary" right thing for you to do?
   _____
   _____
   - What is the "going the extra mile" right thing to do?
   _____
   _____

74

Resource Center

Teaching Tip

Help the students understand that morality involves how we live our lives every day. When you see the students making good moral choices, reflecting on the Church's moral teachings, and acting out of good conscience, make a point of mentioning it. Your acknowledgment may be public or private, depending on the situation. Encourage the students to be on the lookout for examples of everyday Christian morality in their own midst.

Link to the Faith Community

Ask a volunteer from your local Catholic Charities office to speak to the class about efforts to meet the needs of people in your community. Have the students brainstorm ways in which they might support these efforts. How do Catholic Charities workers go the "extra mile"?

Spiritual maturity

About now, you may be saying, "Wait a minute! Faith doesn't make us more free. It just gives us all kinds of new responsibilities and new laws to follow. Who wants that?" This argument sounds logical enough, but let's check it out.

Children have more free time to play than adults. But children, overall, have less freedom than adults. Children can't drive a car, sign contracts, rent an apartment, work at a paid job, stay out all night, or see any movie they want. Adults do have these freedoms. On the other hand, adults have many more responsibilities than children. They have to pay the gasoline, insurance, and maintenance bills on the car. They have to work so many hours a week, and they have to pay bills on time.

Even though adults have more responsibilities than children, most teenagers would rather be treated as adults than as children. To them, the freedom that comes with adulthood is worth the added responsibilities.

The same is true of Christian morality. We can choose to stay at the level of childhood faith, with less freedom and less responsibility. Or we can choose to become spiritually adult, with more freedom and more responsibility. The more Christ-like we become, the more spiritually adult we become! We have more freedom because we see more of reality through the eyes of faith. But we also take on a new level of moral responsibility. More often than not, truly mature Christians choose to go the "extra mile" when it comes to loving God and other people.

F.Y.I.

Spiritually mature Christians are called *saints*. The official process by which the Church recognizes a person as a saint is called *canonization*.

Circle the statement that best describes how you feel right now.
- Faith adds more rules for me to follow and makes "being good" harder.
- Faith gives me a new level of freedom.

Why I feel this way:

_____

_____

Saints are for real ⑤

Many people have the wrong idea about saints. They think the saints were perfect people, people much better than they could ever be. Other people think that saints were dull, boring, unhappy people who hated laughter and who avoided anything fun in life.

Neither image is true. For one thing, saints were human like all of us. They had faults and annoying habits. They fought with their brothers and sisters. Most weren't smarter or more talented than the rest of us. If they became saints, it wasn't because they had an advantage or a head start on goodness. Just like us, they started out as babies, and they got the basic equipment we all get—intelligence and freedom.

On the other hand, saints were anything but dull, boring, or unhappy people who avoided fun. In fact, saints were the happiest, most interesting, and adventuresome kind of people. Saints lived their lives to the fullest.

So what made these people saints? First of all, they worked at being friends with God. Second, they worked hard at imitating Jesus. Third, they had great faith, and they made good moral decisions based on that faith. They did these things one day at a time, just as the rest of us do.

From the saints, we can learn how to be friends with God. Like the saints, we can talk with God through prayer, the Mass, and the sacraments. We can find God in those in need. We can include God in whatever we are doing.

From the saints, we can also learn how we can imitate Jesus in the way we love God the Father and our neighbors. We can learn from the saints how to live life to the fullest and to have real fun in the process. After all, saints were the ones who lived their faith and made it a part of their every moral decision.

Chapter Overview

As a result of our heightened awareness, faith heightens our freedom. But it also increases our responsibility for choices we make. Being a follower of Jesus means imitating Jesus. It means acting in ways that are consistent with the mind and heart of Jesus. In some cases it means going beyond what's right in an ordinary sense. It means doing more, going "the extra mile" beyond what we ordinarily would do.

The Language of Faith

To be *canonized* means that one has been officially declared a saint by the Church. The process involves four basic steps: (1) An individual or group petitions the bishop to consider the person. (2) Experts conduct an investigation of the person's life, writings, and miracles. (3) The Congregation for the Causes of the Saints (in Rome) reviews all relevant documents. (4) The pope issues an official announcement of canonization. On the path to sainthood, a person is first declared Venerable, then Blessed, and finally Saint.

---

2. Ask volunteers to take turns reading aloud the text on page **75** entitled **Spiritual maturity**. Discuss as needed.

Optional

Take a poll of the students. Ask how many would rather be treated as adults and how many would rather be treated as children. Then ask the students to give their reasons for their answer.

3. Ask another volunteer to read aloud the **F.Y.I.** section or allow time for the students to read this section on their own.

Optional

Explain the canonization process. In the first step, the Church conducts an official study of a person's life to determine whether or not it was morally good and holy. If the person passes this test, he or she is officially declared "Venerable" by the Church. In the second step, Church officials must be able to prove that a miracle was worked in the person's name or through the person's intercession. If the person passes this test, he or she is officially declared "Blessed" and is given a feast day on the Church calendar. If Church officials can prove a second miracle was worked in the person's name or through the person's intercession, the person is officially declared a "Saint."

4. Allow time for the students to work alone to complete the **Journal** entry.

5. Ask volunteers to take turns reading aloud **Saints are for real**. Discuss as needed.

1. Draw the students' attention to the **Catechism Connection** at the top of page **76**. Make sure they understand that God is calling each one of them to be a saint.

2. Ask another student to read aloud the F.Y.I. section or allow time for the students to read the section on their own. Perhaps discuss ways that people today might act in heroic, or saintly, ways—especially in areas calling for social justice.

3. Ask a student to read aloud the introduction of **A variety of saints**. Call on other students to take turns reading aloud the paragraphs about specific saints.

4. Ask another volunteer to read aloud the F.Y.I. section, or allow time for the students to read this section on their own.

Optional

Distribute books on the saints and allow time for the students (perhaps working in groups) to find out more about one of the saints and then report their findings to the class.

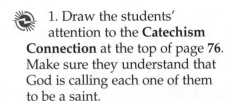

① **Catechism Connection**

"All Christians in any state or walk of life are called to the fullness of Christian life and to the perfection of charity." [LG 40 § 2.] All are called to holiness. . . . (2013)

② **F.Y.I.**

Imitating the saints does not necessarily mean imitating all of their specific actions (such as wearing a hair shirt, whipping ourselves, or living alone in the desert). Certain actions made sense for them, their situation, and their time in history. But their actions might not make sense for us in our situation today.

A variety of saints ③

The Church believes that every person is called by God to holiness. That is why, over the centuries, the Church has honored people of different races, ages, professions, and countries as saints. Here are just a few examples of such people, who lived out their faith in their daily decisions.

Joan of Arc. This French teenager led an army against English invaders and restored King Charles V to his rightful throne.

Francis of Assisi. This Italian youth gave up his wealth to preach God's word to the poor. Francis, who founded the Franciscan order, was also known for his love of animals and all of nature.

Helena. This wealthy empress led an expedition to the Holy Land to recover the true cross of Jesus. She is credited with the conversion of her son, Constantine the Great, who stopped the persecution of Christians by the Roman Empire.

Peter Claver. Born in Spain in 1580, this Jesuit priest served as a missionary in Cartagena, the country that is now Columbia. Black tribespeople from West Africa were shipped to Cartagena in great numbers to be slaves in mines and plantations. Treated more like animals than human beings, the tribespeople were penned up in yards, crowded together, and given no personal care or medical attention. Peter Claver devoted himself to their needs. He brought them medicines and food, bread, brandy, citrus fruits, and tobacco. He visited them, nursed their sick, and treated them with respect and reverence, as brothers and sisters in the Lord.

Martin de Porres. This Peruvian was half Spanish and half black. Although he was a Dominican brother, people often mistreated him because of his mixed race. Instead of becoming resentful about this, Martin spent his life working among Indians and blacks. He fed the hungry, found homes for orphans, and cared for the sick.

Elizabeth Ann Seton. This widow with five children converted from the Episcopalian Church to Catholicism. To earn a living for her family, she started a school in Emmitsburg, Maryland. There, she accepted not only students who could afford to pay the tuition, but also the poor. Elizabeth saw Jesus in the poor and in the uneducated. And so she founded a religious sisterhood, the Sisters of Charity, in the United States. This community was devoted to helping the poor and to teaching.

F.Y.I. ④

In 1975, Pope Paul VI named Elizabeth Seton the first U.S.-born citizen to be proclaimed a saint. The Church celebrates her feast on January 4.

76

<u>Materials</u>
- books on the saints (optional)

Resource Center

The Language of Faith

- A *saint* is someone whose life bears special witness to the gospel message. Saints are people of all ages, national origins, and walks of life. Saints are happy forever with God. The Church honors the saints by celebrating their feast days and by asking for their prayers.

- *Canonization* is the process by which the Catholic Church formally recognizes a deceased person as a saint. Once that person's virtues are publicly recognized, he or she is given a place in the Church's official calendar, or *canon*, of feast days. Many saints of the early Church, and other holy men and women of later years, are not canonized, but we celebrate their virtues with those of all other holy men and women on November 1, the Feast of All Saints.

And prophets, too ⑤

Just as we are all called to be saints, we are all called to be prophets. The word *prophet* comes from a Greek word meaning "to speak out" or "to speak for." A prophet is one who does both. The prophet speaks to all who will listen. The prophet speaks for God. In popular language, a prophet is someone who predicts the future. But in a religious sense, the role of the prophet is to point us to the future.

The authentic prophet who speaks for God calls people forward and calls people back. The Church plays a prophetic role in society. Sometimes the Church challenges society to new levels of holiness. Sometimes it challenges society to turn from injustice and sin.

The Church's prophetic task involves all its other roles. Sometimes the Church is prophetic when it acts as teacher, as when the bishops present a pastoral letter. Sometimes it issues a prophetic challenge to society in its role as servant. The Church's example in caring for the poor, for example, often calls others to share that concern.

Within the Church itself, God often sends prophetic individuals and groups to do the same thing. These individuals challenge us to reach new levels of holiness or call us to turn back from some form of selfishness and injustice.

The role of prophet is not to predict the future but to shape it by speaking for God and to point us in the right direction. To speak out for God and to point society in the right direction is a key role for the Church.

Anyone can serve as a prophet, spreading God's word. In fact, as a disciple of Jesus, you are called to speak out against injustice when you see it. You can challenge your friends and speak out against a prejudice in your school, for example. You can join with others in a public march to support life. You do not need to speak loudly or aggressively. In fact, speaking politely and respectfully may gain better results. You could, for example, quietly tell someone when others aren't around that you did not appreciate his or her joke about homosexuals, that it was insulting and not an appropriate subject matter for jokes.

⑥ Prophetic Voices

Some people have a special calling from God to serve as prophets. See if you recognize any of the following people who are considered prophets. For the Old Testament prophets, check the introductions to their books.

G Amos

D Archbishop Oscar Romero

B Dorothy Day

E Isaiah

F Jeremiah

C John XXIII

A John the Baptist

A. person in the New Testament who called the people to repent and spoke of the coming of the Messiah

B. grew up in Chicago, converted to Catholicism, and founded the Catholic Worker Movement to feed the poor and to house the homeless

C. brought change into the Catholic Church through a council held in 1963, ninety-four years after the first council was held

D. publicly decried the atrocities of the military forces in El Salvador in 1980 and was shot while saying Mass for his speaking out for the poor of El Salvador

E. person in the Old Testament who, as a member of an aristocratic family, spoke out against those who worshipped at the Temple but forgot God's poor; also spoke about "Emmanuel" and the remnant of Israel

F. person in the Old Testament who said that knowing God is to achieve justice for the poor; there were conspiracies against his life in his own town

G. a simple shepherd in the Old Testament who condemned the rich whose business practices and style of life caused great mistreatment of the poor

77

5. Ask for volunteers to take turns reading the section on page **77** entitled **And Prophets, Too**. Discuss the following questions:

- To whom does a prophet speak, and for whom? *(to all who will listen; for God)*

- What is the Church's prophetic role in society? *(challenges society to new levels of holiness; challenges society to turn from injustice and sin)*

- How do individual prophets call us? *(challenge us to reach new levels of holiness or to turn back from some form of selfishness and injustice)*

- How can you serve as a prophet?

6. Have the students form groups of three or four to complete the activity **Prophetic Voices**. Encourage the students to guess if they don't know the correct answers. When everyone has finished, go over the answers in class. Make sure the students understand that a prophet is not someone who foretells the future. A prophet is someone who publicly speaks out about the truth.

The Language of Faith

- *Martyrs* are faithful witnesses who have died for the Christian faith. Some saints are martyrs, but not all martyrs are canonized saints. The Church survived despite years of persecution largely because martyrs faced death rather than deny their faith. We can pray in gratitude for saints like Stephen, the first Christian martyr, and Felicity and Perpetua, two early martyrs.

- To be *sanctified* means to be made holy, to be changed by God's grace into a person who truly loves God and others through his or her thoughts, words, and actions. All of us are called to holiness. The Church helps us achieve this loving response to God through the celebration of the sacraments, the teachings of Jesus, and the gatherings of the faith community.

1. If possible, take the class to a church or a chapel that has the stations of the cross. Assign fourteen students to read the prayers found in their workbooks for each station (**A Disciple's Way of the Cross**, pages 78–80). At the end of each of the readings, pray together the Prayer for the Way of the Cross on page **105** of the student text.

We adore you, O Christ, and we bless you,
because by your holy cross
you have redeemed the world.

After the prayers, allow time for meditations and personal comment.

① A Disciple's Way of the Cross

First Station—Jesus Is Condemned.

"As for yourselves, beware; for they will hand you over to councils; and you will be beaten in syna-gogues; and you will stand before governors and kings because of me, as a testimony to them."

—Mark 13:9

Mohandas Gandhi was a lawyer who in the 1900s fasted in protest against the treatment of the untouchables in India and to end religious strife there. He was imprisoned on several occasions for his nonviolent protests to gain India's independence from Great Britain. Gandhi was assassinated on January 30, 1948.

Second Station—Jesus Takes His Cross.

[Jesus] called the crowd with his disciples, and said to them, "If any want to become my followers, let them deny themselves and take up their cross and follow me."

—Mark 8:34; Matthew 16:24; Luke 9:23

Arthur Ashe was an African American who broke into the white world of tennis. Ashe worked for racial equality. He challenged the government's weak efforts toward AIDS research after contracting AIDS from a blood transfusion. Arthur Ashe died in 1995 after a twelve-year battle with AIDS.

Third Station—Jesus Falls the First Time.

"Blessed are you when people revile you and persecute you and utter all kinds of evil against you false-ly on my account."

—Matthew 5:11

Steven Biko fought against the apartheid system of South Africa. The government claimed he and oth-ers "accidentally fell down the steps or slipped on a bar of soap in the shower," which resulted in their death in 1977. The movie *Cry Freedom* is based on his life. Nelson Mandela spent twenty-eight years in jail for his stand against apartheid. He was released in 1990 and was elected president of South Africa on May 10, 1994.

Fourth Station—Jesus Meets His Mother.

"And the king will answer them, 'Truly I tell you, just as you did it to one of the least of these who are members of my family, you did it to me.'"

—Matthew 25:40

Mother Teresa of Calcutta founded the Sisters of the Missionaries of Charity, whose main mission is to teach the poor children, to nurse the sick, and to prepare the dying for a happy death. The sisters' work has expanded to the larger cities in the United States. Mother Teresa has received many awards including the Nobel Peace Prize in 1979.

Fifth Station—Jesus Is Helped by Simon of Cyrene.

"It will not be so among you; but whoever wishes to be great among you must be your servant . . . "

—Matthew 20:26

Amnesty International, a worldwide organization that involves musicians, actors, athletes, writers, teachers, students, doctors, and many others, acts on the conviction that governments must not deny individuals their basic human rights. Their main action on behalf of prisoners of conscience is through letter-writing campaigns.

Peace Troupe is a grassroots collective of artists, performers, and activists dedicated to nonviolent con-flict resolution.

78

Resource Center

Chapter Overview

Just as all people are called by God to become morally and spiritually mature, so we all are called to holiness. Such holiness means making decisions and acting in ways that are consistent with self-love, love of others, and love of God.

Link to the Faith Community

The *Way of the Cross* is a special devotion that helps us recall Jesus' suffering, death, and resurrection. There are fourteen traditional stations, or opportunities for meditative prayer, beginning with Jesus' being condemned to death and ending with his being laid in the tomb. Some parishes also include a fifteenth station that shows Jesus' resurrection. Although a person can follow the Way of the Cross privately at any time, public devotions are often held during the Lenten Season.

Sixth Station—Veronica Wipes the Face of Jesus.

"You are the light of the world. A city built on a hill cannot be hid. In the same way, let your light shine before others, so that they may see your good works and give glory to your Father in heaven."

—Matthew 5:14, 16

Jean Donovan, who, despite being from a privileged, successful family in Ohio, having a master's degree in economics and excellent career opportunities, decided in 1978 to join a team of missionaries in El Salvador to educate, feed, nurse, and wipe the faces of the many children of El Salvador. Jean Donovan and three missionary sisters were raped and shot in December 1980.

Seventh Station—Jesus Falls the Second Time.

"But before all this occurs, they will arrest you and persecute you; they will hand you over to synagogues and prisons, and you will be brought before kings and governors because of my name."

—Luke 21:12

Dorothy Day, a convert to Catholicism, was cofounder of the Catholic Worker Movement and a major figure in the Catholic peace movement and the growth of pacifism in the United States. Her commitment to social justice, especially to the poor, was evident by her six imprisonments for civil rights.

Eighth Station—Jesus Speaks to the Women of Jerusalem.

Then Jesus said, "Father, forgive them; for they do not know what they are doing."

—Luke 23:34

Rosa Parks led the civil rights crusade in 1955 by her refusal to give up her seat on a bus in Alabama. Susan B. Anthony worked for almost 60 years for women's right to vote in the United States. This right was granted in 1920 through the 19th amendment to the Constitution.

Ninth Station—Jesus Falls the Third Time.

"When they bring you to trial and hand you over, do not worry beforehand about what you are to say; but say whatever is given you at that time, for it is not you who speak, but the Holy Spirit."

—Mark 13:11

Christopher Reeve, Superman to many, is paralyzed from his neck down following an equestrian accident that happened in May 1995. He is an inspiration to all because of the value that he places on his life despite his paralysis. He is on the board of directors for the American Paralysis Association and is also supportive of the environment, AIDS, and other noteworthy causes.

79

Optional

Suggest to the students that they and their family members nominate people as Saints of the Day. Ask each student to interview his or her family members and ask them to suggest the names of people whose daily lives give witness to the qualities that saints possess: dedication to God, a display of grace, positive qualities and actions. Allow time in class for the students to present and discuss their nominees.

Stations of the Cross

Scriptural

1. Jesus prays in the Garden of Olives
2. Jesus is betrayed by Judas and arrested.
3. Jesus is condemned by the Sanhedrin.
4. Jesus is denied by Peter.
5. Jesus is condemned by Pontius Pilate.
6. Jesus is scourged and crowned with thorns.
7. Jesus is made to carry the cross.
8. Simon of Cyrene helps Jesus.
9. Jesus meets the women of Jerusalem.
10. Jesus is crucified.
11. Jesus promises the kingdom to the thief who repents.
12. Jesus speaks to his mother and his friend John.
13. Jesus dies on the cross.
14. Jesus is laid in the tomb.

1. As a class, discuss the **Something to talk about** questions on page **80**. If you choose, have the students remain in the church or the chapel while the class discusses the questions. Make sure the students realize that YES, junior high students can be saints.

Optional

To help the students appreciate the diversity of saints and prophets, share stories of one or two saints or prophets from other countries or cultures, such as Saint Martin de Porres of Peru (of African-European ancestry); Blessed Kateri Tekakwitha, a Native American; or Saint Stephen, the King of Hungary. You might consult *Saint of the Day* by Leonard Foley for information.

Tenth Station—Jesus Is Stripped of His Garments.

"When they hand you over, do not worry about how you are to speak or what you are to say; for what you are to say will be given to you at that time. . . ."
—Matthew 10:19

Joan of Arc was an illiterate, teenage peasant girl who led French troops against English forces in 1430. She was taken prisoner and held in jail for about a year, where she was tried as a heretic, sentenced to death, and excommunicated. At the age of nineteen, she was burned at the stake. The Church canonized her a saint in 1920 and two years later declared her the patroness of France.

Eleventh Station—Jesus Is Nailed to the Cross.

"Very truly, I tell you, the one who believes in me will also do the works that I do and, in fact, will do greater works than these, because I am going to the Father."
—John 14:12

Martin Luther King Jr. was the voice of the nonviolent civil rights movement in the United States. From 1957 through January 1963, seventeen unsolved bombings of black churches and homes of civil rights leaders occurred. Lunch counter sit-ins and marches on city hall resulted in numerous arrests of Reverend King and other black people. Martin Luther King's belief was "nonviolence or nonexistence." He was assassinated on June 4, 1968.

Twelfth Station—Jesus Dies on the Cross.

"You have heard that it was said, 'You shall love your neighbor and hate your enemy.' But I say to you, Love your enemies and pray for those who persecute you. . . ."
—Matthew 5:43–44

Archbishop Oscar Romero of El Salvador, who because of his public announcements decrying the atrocities of the military forces in El Salvador, was put on the death list. On March 23, 1980, while saying Mass, Archbishop Romero was shot. No one has ever been found guilty or charged for his death nor the deaths of Jean Donovan and the three missionary sisters who were killed in December 1980.

Thirteenth Station—Jesus Is Taken Down from the Cross.

And Jesus said to him, "Foxes have holes, and birds of the air have nests; but the Son of Man has nowhere to lay his head."
—Matthew 8:20

Harriet Tubman was the "Moses" of her people, bringing black people out of slavery into freedom through the Underground Railroad system. She had $40,000 put out on her life because of her underground work.

Fourteenth Station—Jesus Is Placed in the Tomb.

"This is my commandment, that you love one another as I have loved you."
—John 15:12

Let us remember all who have worked for justice and for those who continue to work for justice but don't necessarily make the headlines—people like you and me who in our daily lives see wrongs and try to make right, those who proclaim the "gospel of life" to protect the least among us so that all may rise and enter the kingdom of heaven.

(1) **SOMETHING TO TALK ABOUT**

1. Can people your age be saints? Why or why not?

2. Do you know anyone your age or older whom you would consider to be a saint? Why do you feel this way? Describe the person (no names, please).

80

Resource Center

Multicultural Link

Explain that the cross is a very old symbol shown in many different forms by people from different countries and Churches. All forms of the cross show love and devotion that Christians throughout the world have for Jesus and how they are united with one another because of Jesus. The form of the cross that the children are probably most familiar with is the Roman cross. If possible, bring in examples or pictures of other crosses, such as the Celtic cross, the Maltese cross, or the Greek cross. Invite the students to bring in different or unique crosses that their families may have at home.

 **Gather for prayer**

Reflection

 So then you are no longer strangers and aliens, but you are citizens with the saints and also members of the household of God. . . . " (Ephesians 2:19)

Briefly discuss ways that young people today can be saints.

Do I truly believe that God is calling me to be a saint? Why?
_____
_____
_____

Here are some ways I can be more fully alive and grow in holiness:
_____
_____
_____

Jesus,
Help me see beyond externals and see reality through the eyes of faith.
Help me grow spiritually mature and "go the extra mile" in loving others.
Help me look to the saints as inspiration for my everyday life and ask their help in making moral decisions.
Amen.

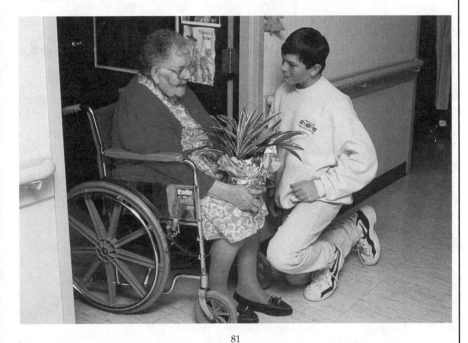

81

2. Gather the students, with their books and a pen/pencil, in the designated prayer corner or sacred space. If fire laws permit, light a candle.

3. After the students have become settled, ask a volunteer to read Ephesians 2:19 (page **81**). Invite the students to reflect silently on what they have heard.

4. After a brief period of silence, ask the students to discuss ways that young people today can be saints.

 5. Allow time for the students to complete the **Journal** entries.

6. Pray together the prayer.

> **Optional**

Conclude the **Reflection** by listening to or by singing an appropriate song.

- "Blest Are They" by David Haas from *Gather (Comprehensive)* (GIA), *Glory & Praise* (OCP [NALR]), *Today's Missal* (OCP).

- "City of God" by Dan Schutte from *Glory & Praise* (OCP [NALR]), *Gather (Comprehensive)* (GIA), *Today's Missal* (OCP).

- "Come to the Water" by John Foley from *Glory & Praise* (OCP [NALR]), *Today's Missal* (OCP), *Gather (Comprehensive)* (GIA).

- "Here I Am, Lord," by Dan Schutte from *Glory & Praise* (OCP [NALR]), *Gather (Comprehensive)* (GIA), *Today's Missal* (OCP).

- "We Are Called" by David Haas from *Gather (Comprehensive)* (GIA).

Chapter Overview

The chapter introduces the students to some of the canonized saints of the Church and helps them realize that these were ordinary people like us who worked at being friends with God and who worked hard at imitating Jesus. They had great faith, and they made good moral decisions based on that faith. They became saints one day at a time, just as the rest of us do. In our journey toward moral maturity, we can look to the saints as role models and ask for their help.

1. Remind the students to do the **Homework** and to review the chapter for the next class. Make available books on the saints to help the students with the homework.

Optional

There will be a short quiz at the beginning of the next class.

Multimedia Resources

Heroes of Faith, "Jean Donovan," produced by Heart of the Nation (video) (BROWN-ROA, 1-800-922-7696).

Heroes of Faith, "St. Francis of Assisi," produced by Heart of the Nation (video) (BROWN-ROA, 1-800-922-7696).

Heroes of Faith, "Dorothy Day," produced by Heart of the Nation (video) (BROWN-ROA, 1-800-922-7696).

Heroes of Faith, "Martin Luther King, Jr.," produced by Heart of the Nation (video) (BROWN-ROA, 1-800-922-7696).

Jesus in My Life Today, produced by Robert Blaskey (video) (BROWN-ROA, 1-800-922-7696).

Stories of the Human Spirit, "The Helper and the Homeless Woman," produced by ACTA Publications (video) (BROWN-ROA, 1-800-922-7696).

HOMEWORK ①

Find the names of the following saints and prophets in the word-search puzzle.

Amos	Dominic	Jean Donovan	Martin de Porres	Paul
Andrew	Dorothy Day	Jeremiah	Martin Luther	Peter
Anne	Elizabeth Seton	Joan of Arc	King Jr.	Rita
Arthur Ashe	Frances Cabrini	John	Mary	Rosa Parks
Brigid	Francis of Assisi	John the Baptist	Monica	Rose
Catherine	Gandhi	John XXIII	Mother Teresa	Stephen
Charles Lwanga	Gregory	Kateri Tekakwitha	Nelson Mandela	Steven Biko
Christopher Reeve	Harriet Tubman	Lucy	Nicolas	Teresa of Ávila
Clare	Helena	Luke	Oscar Romero	Valentine
David	Isaiah	Mark	Patrick	

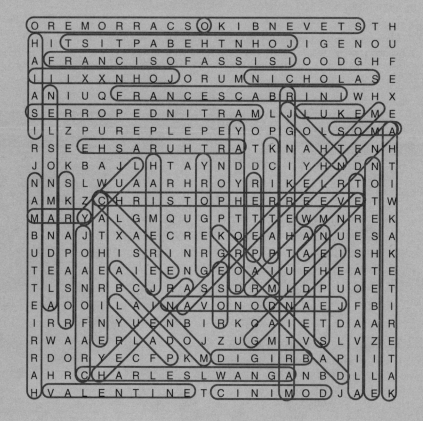

82

Matching

_____ 1. Blaise
_____ 2. Charles Lwanga
_____ 3. Clare
_____ 4. Elizabeth Seton
_____ 5. Frances Cabrini
_____ 6. Francis of Assisi
_____ 7. Helena
_____ 8. Joan
_____ 9. Kateri Tekakwitha
_____ 10. Martin de Porres
_____ 11. Patrick
_____ 12. Paul
_____ 13. Peter
_____ 14. Rose
_____ 15. Teresa Ávila

A. Patron saint of Ireland

B. U.S. citizen, founder of hospitals

C. Known for his poverty and his love of all creatures

D. First U.S.-born saint, founded schools

E. Native American, beatified in 1980

F. Dominican of Peru, patron of social justice

G. Martyr of Uganda

H. Friend of Saint Francis, founder of Franciscan community for women

I. Reformer of religious communities, Doctor of the Church

J. First leader of the Christian Church

K. Apostle to the Gentiles (non-Jews)

L. Known for the blessing of throats on his feast day

M. Dominican of Lima, Peru, first New World native-born saint

N. French heroine who led an army against English invaders

O. Empress, mother of Constantine the Great

Answers to the Homework

Matching

1. L	5. B	9. E	13. J
2. G	6. C	10. F	14. M
3. H	7. O	11. A	15. I
4. D	8. N	12. K	

Name: _____ Date: _____

7: What Do You See?
Review Quiz

True or False

_____ 1. Faith helps us to see and to value reality as God sees and values it.

_____ 2. Once we see things the way Christ does, we reach a new level of moral responsibility.

_____ 3. Saints were perfect people.

_____ 4. Only certain people are called to holiness.

_____ 5. The first American-born citizen to be declared a saint was Peter Claver.

_____ 6. Only adults can be saints.

Fill in the Blanks

1. Jesus saw reality through the eyes of _____.

2. Spiritual eyesight means seeing beyond what is actually there and also seeing the _____ that is there.

3. Being a follower of Jesus means _____ Jesus.

4. The process whereby the Church officially recognizes someone as a saint is called _____.

5. Calling people forward and calling people back is the function of a _____.

6. Like the saints, we can talk with God through _____, _____, and _____.

BROWN-ROA, a division of Harcourt Brace & Company

7: What Do You See?
Review Quiz

Essay

1. Explain the formula Faith Knowledge = Christ-like Freedom = Christ-like Responsibility.

2. List and explain the qualities that help make a person a saint and those that help make a person a prophet.

3. Select a problem that exists in your community. List and explain the actions to which a prophet might call people in order to improve conditions.

BROWN-ROA, a division of Harcourt Brace & Company

8

Lesson Procedure

Academic Goals: To understand ways the Church helps us on our moral journey throughout life and to review the basic content of the course.

Attitudinal Goals: To appreciate the Sacrament of Reconciliation as an aid to moral maturity and to grow in our desire to become the best people possible.

1. Go over the chapter 7 **Homework** answers, found on pages **82–83**.

2. Review chapter 7 by giving the students a quiz. Reproduce page **83A** and/or page **83B** and give one to each student. After the students have completed the quiz, collect them to correct later. If you wish, correct the quizzes in class with the students.

Optional

As the students take the review quiz, collect their textbooks and journals. Scan the pages to make sure the students are completing the **Journal** activities. Also scan for indications of problems that should be addressed.

3. Allow time for the students to work alone to complete the **Imagine this** activity on page **84**. Discuss the students' answers in class. Make sure the students realize that people are meant to be with other people. They are not meant to go through life alone.

---

8 ① *Discuss homework assignment.* ② *Give students the review quiz.*

You're Not Alone

③ ☁ **Imagine this** ☁

Write your answers to each of the following situations. Then discuss your answers in class.

1. You're stranded on a desert island. You have a shipload of food, clothing, and furniture. But there are no other survivors. What would your world be like? What would be the advantages of living alone? What would be the disadvantages?

_____
_____
_____
_____
_____
_____

2. NASA has chosen you to be the first person to land on Mars. Other astronauts will be with you in the rocket that takes off from earth. But these astronauts must stay behind in the space lab while you take a smaller rocket to Mars. Your journey alone will last two months. What would you like about this mission? What would you dislike? Why?

_____
_____
_____
_____
_____

3. You've discovered a treasure map that shows you the exact location of a lost civilization in the deepest wilds of Africa. You know that there is a fortune in diamonds to be found at this site. You also know that getting to the lost city will be very dangerous. No one who has started for the treasure has lived to tell about it. Before you set out, you are given a choice. You can try to make it alone, depending on your own intelligence and willpower, supplies, and maps. (That way, the treasure will be all yours.) Or you can travel with an organized group. (This would probably be safer, but you'd have to split the treasure with everyone in the group.) Which choice would you make? Why?

_____
_____
_____
_____
_____

84

Chapter 7 Quiz Answers

True or False		**Fill in the Blanks**	
1. T	4. F	1. faith	4. canonization
2. T	5. F	2. value	5. prophet
3. F	6. F	3. imitating	6. prayer, Mass, sacraments (any order)

Essay

1. In the formula *Faith Knowledge = Christ-like Freedom = Christ-like Responsibility*, we are adding faith to the formula studied earlier (*Knowledge = Freedom = Responsibility*). Once we see things the way Christ does, we reach a new level of moral responsibility. We are expected to do more, to live out our faith in charity, which is expressed in the New Law, the law of love, grace, and freedom.

84

The real journey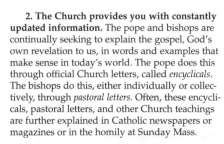

You may not be stranded on a desert island or flying alone to Mars or going on a solo expedition to the African interior. But the fact is, you *are* on a long journey—the journey toward moral maturity. Right now, that journey may seem endlessly complicated and very frightening. After all, it's brand new territory. You've never been there before. You'll have to make decisions you've never made before.

The good news is that none of us are alone on this journey. God has provided us with a group of friends who want to travel with us. That group is called the Church.

There are many advantages to traveling with the Church as you journey through life. Let's look at some of them.

1. The Church provides you with the experience and faith of two thousand years. The Church's laws and teachings are like a map, or a guidebook, that provides you with a new perspective—the eyes of faith. Church teachings and laws aren't there to take away your fun or to give you a hard time. Instead, the laws are like trail markers, pointing out good paths and warning you of harmful ones. They exist to make your journey easier, not more difficult. They don't take away your freedom to choose, but they can save you a lot of time in trying to figure out how to use that freedom.

Sometimes people within the Church or outside the Church have tried to interpret Jesus' teaching differently than he intended. When Jesus was in earthly form, he often defended his teaching against these false teachers. He also warned the apostles and disciples to be alert for such false teaching. They must defend or maintain the true meaning in Jesus' teaching and protect the rest of the Church against these errors.

2. The Church provides you with constantly updated information. The pope and bishops are continually seeking to explain the gospel, God's own revelation to us, in words and examples that make sense in today's world. The pope does this through official Church letters, called *encyclicals*. The bishops do this, either individually or collectively, through *pastoral letters*. Often, these encyclicals, pastoral letters, and other Church teachings are further explained in Catholic newspapers or magazines or in the homily at Sunday Mass.

85

---

4. Ask volunteers to take turns reading aloud the section on page **85** entitled **The real journey**. The section continues onto page **86**.

page **85** onto page **86**

Optional

Matthew's Gospel is the only Gospel that uses the word *church*. Have the students read ***Matthew 16:13–19***. In this passage Jesus appoints Peter head of his future Church. Peter's authority comes not from himself but from Jesus; it is a spiritual authority, unlike the temporal authority of kings, presidents, and other secular leaders. Catholic tradition identifies Peter as the first bishop of Rome, a title given to each pope as Peter's successor.

Optional

In order to form their conscience properly, the students must be reminded frequently of the cornerstones of Christian morality. Take time to review the Great Commandment, the Golden Rule, the Ten Commandments, and the Beatitudes with the students. Point out the moral education contained in the Sunday Mass readings. Summarize, in age-appropriate language, moral statements made by the pope and the bishops.

---

2. From the saints, we can learn how to be friends with God. Like the saints, we can talk with God through prayer, the Mass, and the sacraments. We can find God in those in need. We can include God in whatever we are doing. From the saints, we can also learn how we can imitate Jesus in the way we love God the Father and our neighbors. We can learn from the saints how to live life to the fullest and to have real fun in the process. After all, saints were the ones who lived their faith and made it a part of their every moral decision. And as a prophet, we are called to spread God's word. As a disciple of Jesus, we are called to speak out against injustice when we see it.

3. Answers may vary.

1. Have students continue reading the section on page **86** entitled **The real journey**. Discuss as needed. Share with the students why the Church has been an important part of your own moral journey.

Optional

To clarify the Church's teaching on moral issues, invite your pastor or another knowledgeable parish minister to address the students. Invite the students to compose a list of questions in advance. The questions might be rooted in the material you are studying or may be prompted by events in the news (for example, students may be curious about the Church's view of such practices as cloning). Work with your guest speaker ahead of time to make sure he or she can respond to the students' questions in an age-appropriate and doctrinally-sound manner.

①

When the pope and bishops teach under certain conditions, what they say becomes infallible teaching from the Church. *Infallible teaching* means that it is without error. In order for a teaching to be infallible, four criteria must be met:

- The bishops united with the pope must act as supreme pastors and teachers of all Christians.
- The pope (and the bishops in union with the pope) must use his/their supreme apostolic authority.
- The subject matter of the teaching must concern faith and morals.
- The pope must expressly indicate that the doctrine is to be held definitively by all.

Although the pope can profess an infallible teaching by himself, the more common way is for the pope and the bishops to teach through an ecumenical council. They discuss a particular issue and then develop a statement that presents their official teaching to the whole Church as being infallible.

Together the pope and bishops are called the *magisterium*. (*Magisterium* is a Latin word meaning "teaching office.") It is the job of the magisterium to "maintain" truth in all teachings. When there is a dispute over a teaching today, we look to the magisterium to get the official interpretation, much the way the early Christians looked to Peter and the other apostles.

3. The Church provides you with a community of friends. Many people consider their faith a private matter, something between themselves and God. However, we can't really be a community of disciples unless we're willing to share with one another about our common friendship with Jesus. How about yourself? Do you find it difficult and embarrassing to discuss your faith, your prayer life, your feelings about God, the problems you have following Jesus? Most teens do. Yet this sharing is exactly what a community of disciples has in common. We support and encourage each other through sharing and we help each other grow. Learning to be open and willing to talk about your faith with other believers, especially with those your own age, is one of the most important ways you'll need to grow in the coming years.

True friends don't judge you or bully you into doing wrong. They help and advise and warn you of dangers. You can lean on them. You can depend on them. But you remain free to make your own choices. In the Church, your friends walk with you, warn you if you wander off, and pull you out of quicksand if you fall into it. They cheer you up and even carry you on their shoulders if you can't keep going on your own.

4. The Church provides you with many opportunities to communicate with God. Our Christian journey, begun in baptism, is strengthened by the sacramental life of the Church. The Mass, the sacraments, and the spiritual practices of the Church help put you in touch with God. From this communion with God, you can find the strength and courage you need to make and live up to hard choices.

86

Resource Center

Chapter Overview

The Church aids us in several important ways as we journey through life, seeking to make right choices. The Church equips us with faith to see the path we should follow. Church teachings and laws provide a "map" that can guide us in times of moral uncertainty. The Church gives us continual strength through the Mass and sacraments. The Church also provides us with concerned and helpful traveling companions to encourage us, warn us, and even carry us if need be.

The Language of Faith

- The *magisterium* is the teaching authority of the Church, exercised by the bishops together with the pope. The Holy Spirit guides and directs the teachings of these successors of the apostles, keeping the Church faithful to the truth.

- *Infallible* means "incapable of error." Because the Holy Spirit guides the Church, the Church's teaching is infallible in certain matters of faith and morals when the pope or the bishops in union with the pope proclaim by a definitive act that a doctrine of faith or morals is to be embraced as a matter of faith.

② Precepts of the Church

How can each of the following Church laws help you keep traveling toward moral maturity? Write your answers here. Then discuss them in class.

1. You shall attend Mass on Sundays and on holy days of obligation and rest from servile labor. (See page 98.)

_____
_____
_____
_____
_____

2. You shall confess your sins at least once a year.

_____
_____
_____
_____
_____

3. You shall receive the Sacrament of the Eucharist at least during the Easter Season.

_____
_____
_____
_____
_____

4. You shall observe the days of fasting and abstinence established by the Church. (See page 98.)

_____
_____
_____
_____
_____

5. You shall help provide for the needs of the Church.

_____
_____
_____
_____
_____

③ **F.Y.I.** ④

Class discussion.

The Easter Season extends from Easter Sunday to Pentecost, a period of fifty days.

87

2. Have the students form groups of three. Then allow time for them to complete the **Precepts of the Church** activity on page **87**. Point out that they may turn to page **103** in the text for more information about holy days of obligation and the prescribed days of fasting and abstinence.

3. As a class, discuss each of the precepts of the Church.

4. Draw the students' attention to the **F.Y.I.** section, which explains the Easter Season.

Background

The Precepts of the Church: These "commandments of the Church," as they are sometimes called, have existed in some form since the fourth century. The number and content of the *precepts* (a word that means "teachings") has varied throughout the years, and different lists are honored in different countries. Throughout Church history the number of precepts has ranged from five to ten. The precepts of the Church, which apply to all Catholics, have never been given the status of law. The precepts of the Church spell out specific behaviors that are expected of all Catholics. These behaviors are the minimum that Church members must do to show their Catholic identity.

1. Ask volunteers to take turns reading aloud **It's up to you** on page **88**.

 2. Draw the students' attention to the **Catechism Connection**. Point out that the pope and the bishops are together called the *Magesterium*, which means "official teachers" of the Church. They have the responsibility to teach the good news of Jesus and to guide Catholics in moral decisions.

 3. Allow time for the students to work alone to complete the **Journal** entry.

4. Ask volunteers to take turns reading aloud **When we goof**. Make sure the students realize that God doesn't impose unrealistic goals on us. God knows that we are not perfect and that sometimes we will fail or make mistakes. What is important is that we learn from our mistakes, correct them, and keep striving for holiness.

 5. Distribute Bibles. Have the students work alone to complete the **Scripture Search**.

6. As a class, discuss the three **Something to talk about** questions. Make sure the students understand that no matter what they do wrong, God will always take them back if that's what they want.

Materials
• Bibles

It's up to you

Up to now, belonging to the Church has been a choice made by your parents for you. It started with their decision to enroll you as a member of the Church through Baptism. Chances are, it has been mostly their decision that you get to Mass, attend religion classes, and follow the basic practices of Church teaching. But now you are old enough and mature enough to begin to recognize on your own the value of belonging to the Church. You can see that belonging to the Church doesn't take away your freedom. It makes you truly free. You can realize that the Church doesn't do your thinking for you, but it helps you grow up and assume real responsibility for your choices.

If you aren't mature enough to see the truth of this, no arguments are going to convince you. But if you are ready to begin on the moral journey through adulthood, no arguments are necessary. "Going it alone" won't make much sense to you. Traveling with the Church will make sense. Deciding to travel with the Church may very well be the first and most important adult moral choice you make. It's up to you now.

Catechism Connection

The Roman Pontiff and the bishops, as authentic teachers, preach to the People of God the faith which is to be believed and applied in moral life. It is also encumbent on them to pronounce on moral questions that fall within the natural law and reason. [2050]

③

Belonging to the Church is important to me because:

_____
_____
_____
_____
_____

When we goof ④

Unfortunately, most journeys are not without problems. The same is true of the journey toward moral maturity. All of us misuse our freedom sometimes. We make wrong choices. We go against our conscience. We don't live up to our responsibilities. But—in the eyes of God and the Church—even when we goof, all is not lost.

This good news is found in the parable Jesus told about the forgiving father (which is also known as the parable of the prodigal son). The parable teaches us everything we need to know about sin and forgiveness. The central part in the story is played by the father. The father never stops loving and caring for his son no matter how ungrateful the son is or how badly he acts, no matter how long the son stays away. The father is always there looking and waiting. When the son does return, the father doesn't impose huge punishments. He doesn't bawl out the son or say "I told you so." Instead, the father gives the son a big hug and has a party to celebrate his return.

scripture Search ⑤

Read the parable of the forgiving father (Luke 15:11–32). Summarize it here:

A father welcomes his son back after the son left his home and spent all his inheritance.

_____
_____

SOMETHING TO TALK ABOUT ⑥

1. What does the parable tell us about the nature of sin?
2. What does the parable tell us about how God acts after we ask forgiveness for our sins?
3. Why do you think the father in the parable doesn't punish his son?

Resource Center

Background

Throughout Church history different symbols have come to represent the contrition, peace, and forgiveness of Reconciliation. Among such symbols are a dove with an olive branch, tears or raindrops, ashes, sackcloth, keys, a heart, and a rose.

Scripture Background

Luke 15:11–32 contains the parable in which a father joyfully welcomes home his repentant son. Instead of dealing with the son as his sins deserve, the father reinstates him to his place in the family and orders a feast to be held in his honor. The reconciliation is made more poignant by the fact that the son has truly repented his sins and has decided to change his life.

Link to Liturgy

Remind the students that at the beginning of Mass, we as a parish community recall God's mercy and admit our sinfulness. During this part of the Mass, called the penitential rite, we sometimes pray the I Confess Prayer. (See page **98**.)

The right road 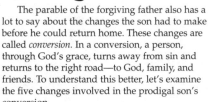 ⑦

The parable of the forgiving father also has a lot to say about the changes the son had to make before he could return home. These changes are called *conversion*. In a conversion, a person, through God's grace, turns away from sin and returns to the right road—to God, family, and friends. To understand this better, let's examine the five changes involved in the prodigal son's conversion.

1. The first thing the son had to do was "come to his senses." He had to recognize his sinful state. He had to realize just how bad things were and how unnecessary it was to continue living like that.
2. The prodigal son had to admit that his problem was his own doing. He had to accept full responsibility for his wrong choices.
3. The son had to be sorry, not just sorry for himself, but sorry for all the wrong he had done.
4. The son had to be willing to do whatever was necessary to correct things. (In the parable, the son decides to work for his father in order to pay back the money he lost.)
5. Lastly, the son had to act. He actually had to go home, admit his sinfulness, and ask his father's forgiveness. Even though the father had already forgiven the son and welcomed him back before the son said anything, the son still felt the need to confess his sinfulness.

SOMETHING TO TALK ABOUT ⑧

1. Do you think the son ever again left home and squandered his father's money? Why?
2. Suppose the son did make the same mistake again. How do you think his father would respond then?
3. Does God give us second and third and fourth chances? Does God ever give up on us? Why do you think this?

Chapter Overview

The chapter assures students that God loves us and welcomes us back home even when we fail or make mistakes. The Sacrament of Reconciliation is a special help to conversion, to turning away from sin and starting over. Such conversion, which is explained according to the parable of the prodigal son, consists of five elements:

- We know that we are wrong;
- We admit our responsibility for our wrong choice;
- We are sorry for what we've done;
- We ask for forgiveness; and
- We are willing to make amends.

Background

Examination of Conscience: The practice of prayerfully reviewing one's life has been part of Christian spirituality from the earliest days. At some time in the Church's history there has been an overemphasis on the legalistic aspects of sin, leading to the development of rigid formulas ("laundry lists") for examination of conscience. Today the emphasis has returned to a more balanced reflection on one's sins and failings with the firm intention to do better. Emphasize that during an examination of conscience, we should consider not only our relationship with God but also our relationships with other people, including those we do not know personally.

---

7. Ask volunteers to take turns reading aloud the section on page **89** entitled **The right road**. Discuss as needed.

 8. As a class, discuss the three **Something to talk about** questions. Make sure the students realize that God NEVER gives up on us, even when other people do.

Optional

One of the best-known and perhaps most poignant Gospel stories is that of the prodigal son (*Luke 15:11–32*), which expresses how utterly forgiving God is. Have the students read this passage in their Bibles. Also encourage them to reread it whenever they are troubled about having sinned and need to be reassured that God is always ready to forgive them.

Optional

Have the students write confidential letters to family members whom they have hurt in some way recently. Ask the students to apologize in the letters for their wrongdoing and promise to do specific penances. Encourage the students to give their finished letters to the family members.

Optional

When the war in Vietnam ended, many families in the United States welcomed back their loved ones by tying yellow ribbons around trees, a custom started by a popular song. The same custom has also been used to welcome home prisoners of war and hostages. If time permits, have the students make Welcome Home signs to post at home as a reminder to forgive and welcome others back to a loving relationship.

Materials

- Bibles (optional)

1. Ask volunteers to take turns reading aloud **The Sacrament of Reconciliation** on page **90**. Discuss as needed.

 2. Draw the students' attention to the **Catechism Connection**. Make sure the students realize that apologizing to God in private is not enough when we have sinned. Because our sins also divide us from others, we also need to be reconciled with them. This reunion with God and with the Church is officially celebrated in the Sacrament of Reconciliation.

 3. Ask another volunteer to read aloud the **F.Y.I.** section, or allow time for the students to read this section on their own. Perhaps ask the students to describe a communal reconciliation service they have attended. Also ask the students which way they prefer to celebrate the sacrament and why.

 4. As a class, discuss the two **Something to talk about** questions.

Optional

Whenever we gather as a community to celebrate the Sacrament of Reconciliation, we demonstrate our faith in a forgiving and reconciling God. Forgiveness and reconciliation are available to those who are truly sorry for their sins. Find out the date of the next communal celebration of the Sacrament of Reconciliation, and post it in the classroom. Also post the times for individual celebration of the sacrament. Encourage the students to participate with their families.

The Sacrament of Reconciliation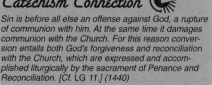

The Sacrament of Reconciliation is modeled after the parable of the forgiving father. First of all, it is a homecoming celebration that focuses on God's ever-present love and forgiveness. The wayward child who "comes home" knows he or she is wrong, admits responsibility, asks for forgiveness, and is ready to do whatever is necessary to correct things.

As you begin your adult journey toward moral maturity, it should be a comfort to know that the Sacrament of Reconciliation will always be there to heal you and to put you back on your feet if you fall. The Sacrament of Reconciliation is always there for you—not to embarrass you or to make you feel guilty, as many people mistakenly think. Instead, the Sacrament of Reconciliation is there to welcome you back if you ever make deliberately wrong choices that cut you off from others, from God, or from your own best self. It's our wrong choices that cause the embarrassment, the guilt, and the pain of being cut off from others. The Sacrament of Reconciliation is there precisely to take away that embarrassment, guilt, and pain. It's to help you once again "come home" and to be friends with others.

Catechism Connection

Sin is before all else an offense against God, a rupture of communion with him. At the same time it damages communion with the Church. For this reason conversion entails both God's forgiveness and reconciliation with the Church, which are expressed and accomplished liturgically by the sacrament of Penance and Reconciliation. [Cf. LG 11.] (1440)

F.Y.I. ✏️ ③

There are several ways to celebrate the Sacrament of Reconciliation. We can confess our sins anonymously to the priest and receive absolution. We can confess our sins face-to-face with the priest and receive absolution. We can participate in a community Reconciliation service with private confession and absolution. In extreme emergencies, the communal celebration can consist of general confession and general absolution.

SOMETHING TO TALK ABOUT ④

1. Why do you think some people feel the Church is a bother rather than a help in making the moral journey?

2. Why do some people dislike the Sacrament of Reconciliation? Are these good reasons or not?

90

Resource Center

The Language of Faith

The *Sacrament of Reconciliation* celebrates God's forgiveness of sin through the Church. This sacrament is also known as *Penance*. The word *reconciliation* means "coming back together" or "making peace."

Background

The Sacrament of Reconciliation: This sacrament has undergone profound changes throughout the centuries of its development, yet at its heart has always been in the gospel call to conversion. The revisions of the *Rite of Penance* begun by the Second Vatican Council raised many questions and affected popular practice. Today the Church reminds us that we are to understand this sacrament only in context: Christ is our central sacrament of reconciliation, working through the Church, whose mission is also to reconcile.

Catechism Background

For more information about the Sacrament of Reconciliation, you may want to read the *Catechism of the Catholic Church* (#s 1422–98).

Summing up the course ⑤

You have learned many things about what's right and what's wrong during the past eight classes. First of all, you've learned that the moral life flows from a personal relationship with Christ. We strive to be good because of God's love for us and our love for God. As the saying goes, "God doesn't make junk." Because of faith you can fully appreciate and honestly love yourself and others.

You begin to see how and why to love your neighbor. The *how* is easy enough: You simply treat others the way you want to be treated. The *why* of loving your neighbor is the hard part. It takes the eyes of faith to recognize that everyone you meet actually *deserves* to be treated with respect and kindness. We can call this ability to see why you should treat each person with respect your *moral sensitivity*.

Finally, being moral means being best friends with God. If you truly love God, then it's important to include God in your plans and decisions. It's important to show God your gratitude and to turn to him for advice and help and forgiveness.

God has given you the Ten Commandments, the law of love, the Golden Rule, the Beatitudes, and the teachings of the Church to help you on your journey. But keep in mind, where you end up on this journey is up to you. If you choose carefully and use your freedom well, you'll create the masterpiece that is inside of you. It's your free choice. You are responsible for the "you" you create!

⑥ *Gather for prayer.*

⑦ 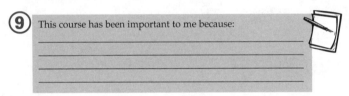 *Reflection*

⑧ *You are my friends if you do what I command you. I am giving you these commands so that you may love one another. (John 15:14, 17)*

Briefly discuss this question: If there was just one thing you could tell others that you learned from this course, what would you want to share? Why?

⑨
This course has been important to me because:
_____
_____
_____
_____

⑩ *Jesus,*
Help me grow closer to you through prayer and frequent reception of the sacraments.
Help me stay close to your Church and its supporting community.
Help me use the freedom you have given me to be the best person I can be.
Amen.

91

---

5. Ask volunteers to take turns reading aloud the section on page **91** entitled **Summing up the course**. Discuss as needed.

6. Gather the students, with their books and a pen/pencil, in the designated prayer corner or sacred space. If fire laws permit, light a candle.

7. After the students have become settled, ask a volunteer to read John 15:14, 17 (page **91**). Invite the students to reflect silently on what they have heard.

8. After a brief period of silence, ask the students to discuss one thing they learned from this course. Encourage everyone to say something.

9. Allow time for the students to complete the **Journal** entry.

10. Pray together the prayer.

Optional

Conclude the **Reflection** by listening to or by singing an appropriate song.

- "Jesus, Heal Us" by David Haas from *Gather (Comprehensive)* (GIA).
- "Pardon Your People" by Carey Landry from *Glory & Praise* (OCP [NALR]).
- "Path of Life" by M. Balhoff, D. Ducote, G. Daigle from *Glory & Praise* (OCP [NALR]).
- "Healer of Our Every Ill" by Marty Haugen from *Gather (Comprehensive)* (GIA).

Background

Because sin affects every relationship we have, it is not a private matter between a person and God. The Sacrament of Reconciliation was celebrated for the first time as public ritual about 150 C.E. At that time the reconciling process was only for the most serious sins and in some places could be used only once in a lifetime. By the seventh century the sacrament began to be celebrated privately in a confessional as many times as the person needed throughout his or her lifetime. The bishops of the Second Vatican Council emphasized that the sacrament involves not only confession and penance but also a celebration of conversion and reconciliation with God and the Christian community.

The Language of Faith

Contrition is sincere sorrow for sin, strong dislike for sin, and the pledge not to sin again. Contrition is the first step in reconciliation with God; without it there can be no forgiveness. God cannot forgive our sins if we are not truly sorry for them or do not want to change our behavior. Contrition is motivated by fear of God's justice and punishment (imperfect contrition) or by love of God and sorrow over offending him (perfect contrition).

1. Remind the students to do the **Homework** and to review the chapter before the last class. Either have a quiz on chapter 8 at this last class or have a final test on the entire course.

Optional

If you plan to have a final test, perhaps give the students the chapter 8 quiz (page **87A**) as additional homework.

HOMEWORK ①

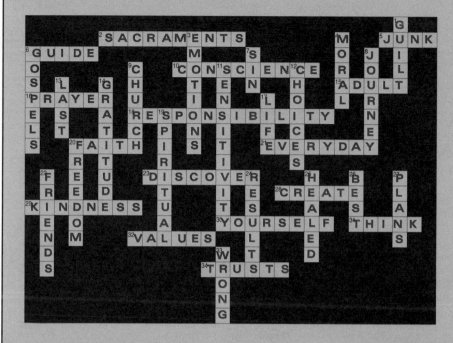

1. You are starting a long (8 down).

2. The teachings and precepts of the Church are rooted in the (6 down).

3. The (2 across) are sources of God's own life-force.

4. When we fail, we are (25 down) in the Sacrament of Reconciliation.

5. The Church provides us with the eyes of (20 across).

6. The Church provides us with a community of (22 down).

7. The Church's sacraments and (19 down) practices put us in touch with God.

8. Belonging to the Church doesn't take away (20 down).

9. The Church helps us assume responsibility for our (12 down).

10. Deciding to travel with the Church is a(n) (15 across) moral choice.

92

Multimedia Resources

A Father and Two Sons, produced by the American Bible Society (IBM-compatible CD-ROM software) (BROWN-ROA, 1-800-922-7696).

Reconciliation: Closing the Gap, produced by BROWN-ROA (video) (BROWN-ROA, 1-800-922-7696).

Stories of the Human Spirit, "The Woman and the Kid in Lincoln Park," produced by ACTA Publications (video) (BROWN-ROA, 1-800-922-7696).

The Prodigal (video) (BROWN-ROA, 1-800-922-7696).

Together in Faith, produced by Salt River Production Group (video) (BROWN-ROA, 1-800-922-7696).

Answers to the Homework

1. journey	13. create	25. emotions
2. gospels	14. discover	26. responsibility
3. sacraments	15. yourself	27. results
4. healed	16. kindness	28. guilt
5. faith	17. sensitivity	29. Sin
6. friends	18. best	30. everyday
7. spiritual	19. plans	31. wrong
8. freedom	20. gratitude	32. prayer
9. choices	21. life	33. last
10. adult	22. guide	34. think
11. junk	23. values	35. Church
12. moral	24. conscience	36. trusts

11. God doesn't make (5 across).

12. The (4 down) life begins with authentic love of self.

13. You are responsible for the "you" you (28 across).

14. From love of self, you (23 across) how and why to love your neighbor.

15. Treat your neighbor as (30 across).

16. Everyone deserves to be treated with respect and (29 across).

17. Our ability to treat others with respect is our moral (11 down).

18. Being moral means being (26 down) friends with God.

19. Being moral means involving God in our (27 down) and decisions.

20. We owe God our (14 down).

21. The moral (17 down) means loving God in practical ways.

22. You have a conscience to (6 across) you.

23. A personalized conscience includes your convictions and (32 across).

24. A mature (10 across) judges good and bad with the mind of Christ.

25. Strong (3 down) can limit your freedom.

26. The flip side of freedom is (18 across).

27. Bad choices sooner or later cause bad (24 down).

28. Bad choices bring a sense of (1 down).

29. (7 down) is selfishness.

30. Most of our moral life is made up of (21 across) decisions.

31. True friends never ask a person to do something that is (33 down).

32. Good advisors and (16 across) can help us make decisions.

33. Snap decisions can have results that (13 down) the rest of our life.

34. We have to discipline ourselves to take time to (31 across).

35. It is important to take the (9 down) seriously.

36. A spiritually mature person loves God above everything else and (34 across) in God's love.

Name: _____   Date: _____

8: You're Not Alone
Review Quiz

True or False

_____ 1. The Church provides you with the eyes of faith.

_____ 2. The sacraments and the spiritual practices of the Church put you in touch with God.

_____ 3. Belonging to the Church takes away most of your freedom.

_____ 4. We strive to be good because of God's love for us and our love for God.

_____ 5. The Sacrament of Reconciliation is intended to make you feel guilty.

_____ 6. When we make wrong choices, there is no way to correct them.

Fill in the Blanks

1. The teachings and _____ of the Church are rooted in the Gospels.

2. The official interpretation of the teachings of the Church is the job of the _____.

3. Deciding to travel with the Church may be the first _____ moral choice you make.

4. Catholics are required to confess their sins at least _____ and to receive Holy Communion at least during _____.

5. The authentic teachers of Catholic morality are _____ and _____.

6. In a true _____, a person turns away from sin and returns to the right road—to God, family, and friends.

8: You're Not Alone
Review Quiz

Essay

1. What are the advantages of traveling with the Church on your moral journey?

2. List the steps of a conversion process.

3. What might be the advantages of using the Sacrament of Reconciliation on a regular basis throughout your life?

BROWN-ROA, a division of Harcourt Brace & Company

The Last Class

1. Begin the class by correcting the chapter 8 **Homework** assignment, found on pages **92–93**.

2. If you gave the students the chapter 8 review quiz as homework, go over the answers now.

3. If you did not assign the quiz for homework, give it to the students now. When the students have finished, collect the quizzes to correct later.

Optional

Distribute copies of the final test and allow time for the students to complete it.

4. After all the tests have been handed in, conclude the course with a party. Use the party as an opportunity to celebrate the time you have spent together and to invite the students to attend another *Crossroads* course.

Your Catholic Heritage

Traditional Prayers

Sign of the Cross
In the name of the Father,
and of the Son,
and of the Holy Spirit.
Amen.

La Señal de la Cruz
Por la señal de la Santa Cruz,
de nuestros enemigos libranos,
Señor, Dios nuestro.
En el nombre del Padre
y del Hijo,
y del Espíritu Santo.
Amén.

The Lord's Prayer

Traditional/Liturgical
Our Father, who art in
   heaven,
hallowed be thy name;
thy kingdom come;
thy will be done on earth
as it is in heaven.
Give us this day our daily
   bread;
and forgive us our
   trespasses
as we forgive those who
trespass against us;
and lead us not into
   temptation,
but deliver us from evil.
(Amen.)
For the kingdom,
the power,
and the glory are yours,
now and for ever.

Contemporary
Our Father in heaven,
hallowed be your name,
your kingdom come,
your will be done,
on earth as in heaven.
Give us today our daily
   bread.
Forgive us our sins
as we forgive those who
   sin against us.
Save us from the time of
   trial
and deliver us from evil.
For the kingdom,
the power,
and the glory are yours,
now and for ever.
Amen.

Scriptural
"Our Father in heaven,
hallowed be your name,
your kingdom come,
your will be done,
on earth as it is in heaven.
Give us today our daily
   bread;
and forgive us our debts
as we forgive our debtors;
and do not subject us to the
   final test,
but deliver us from the evil
   one."
            —*Matthew 6:9–13*
"Father, hallowed be your
   name,
your kingdom come.
Give us each day our daily
   bread
and forgive us our sins
for we ourselves forgive
everyone in debt to us.
And do not subject us to
the final test.
            —*Luke 11:2–4*

94

Chapter 8 Quiz Answers

True or False

1. T   4. T
2. T   5. F
3. F   6. F

Fill in the Blanks

1. spiritual practices
2. magisterium
3. adult
4. once a year, the Easter Season
5. the pope, the bishops (any order)
6. conversion

Essay

1. The advantages of traveling with the Church on our moral journey is that (1) The Church provides us with the experience and faith of two thousand years; (2) The Church provides us with constantly updated information; (3) The Church provides us with a community of friends; (4) The Church provides us with many opportunities to communicate with God.

El Padre Nuestro

Padre nuestro,
que estás en el cielo,
santificado sea tu nombre.
Venga a nosotros tu reino;
hágase tu voluntad en la tierra,
como en el cielo.
Danos hoy nuestro pan
de cada día;
perdona nuestras ofensas,
como también nosotros perdonamos
a los que nos ofenden.
No nos dejes caer en la tentación,
y líbranos del mal.
Amén.

Hail Mary

Hail, Mary, full of grace, the Lord is
    with you!
Blessed are you among women, and
blessed is the fruit of your womb,
    Jesus.
Holy Mary, Mother of God, pray for us
    sinners, now and at the hour of our
    death.
Amen.

Glory to the Father

Glory to the Father,
and to the Son,
and to the Holy Spirit.
As it was in the beginning, is now,
and will be for ever. Amen.

El Ave María

Dios te salve, María;
llena eres de gracia,
el Señor es contigo.
Bendita tú eres entre todas las mujeres,
y bendito es el fruto de tu vientre,
    Jesús.
Santa María, Madre de Dios,
ruega por nosotros pecadores,
ahora, y en la hora de nuestra muerte.
Amén.

La Oración a La Trinidad

Gloria al Padre,
al Hijo,
y al Espíritu Santo;
como era en el principio,
ahora, y siempre,
por los siglos de los siglos.
Amén.

Final Test Answers

True or False

1. F	6. T
2. F	7. F
3. T	8. F
4. F	9. T
5. F	10. F

Word Match

1. R	11. Q
2. S	12. T
3. G	13. B
4. J	14. A
5. P	15. M
6. N	16. I
7. D	17. E
8. H	18. K
9. C	19. F
10. O	20. L

Fill in the Blank

1. objective
2. norms
3. Abba
4. mind, heart (any order)
5. Prejudice
6. praise, trust (any order)
7. God's grace
8. think
9. faith
10. prophet

2. The first step in a conversion process is to "come to your senses," to recognize your sinful state. Second, you need to accept full responsibility for your wrong choices. Next, you need to be truly sorry for all the wrong you have done. Fourth, you must be willing to do whatever is necessary to correct things. And lastly, you need to act on your conversion. After admitting your sinfulness, you must ask forgiveness.

3. Answers may vary.

Short Answers

1. These are the three conditions: (1) The action must be seriously wrong. (2) You must know beforehand that the action is seriously wrong. (3) You must freely and completely choose to act wrongly.

2. First of all, we can't really love others until we love ourselves. Christian morality begins with healthy self-love. Second, Jesus taught that everyone, even our enemy, is our neighbor. Jesus calls us to love everyone.

3. There are three steps to develop your conscience: (1) You have to be honest about what you really think is right and wrong. (2) You have to be open to the advice of good counselors. (3) You have to be critical of the values found in popular culture.

4. There are four advantages of belonging to the Church: (1) The Church provides you with the experience and faith of two thousand years. (2) The Church provides you with constantly updated information in the form of encyclicals, pastoral letters, and other Church teachings. (3) The Church provides you with a community of friends who will support you in making good decisions. (4) The Church provides you with many opportunities to communicate with God (especially through the Mass, the sacraments, and prayer).

Other Prayers

Blessing Before Meals

Bless us, O Lord, and these your gifts which we are about to receive from your goodness.
Through Christ our Lord. Amen.

Thanksgiving After Meals

We give you thanks for all your gifts, almighty God,
living and reigning now and for ever. Amen.

Prayer of Saint Alphonsus Liguori

Grant me the gift of knowledge, so I may know
the things of God and, enlightened by your holy teaching,
may walk without deviation in the path of eternal salvation.

Act of Contrition

My God,
I am sorry for my sins with all my heart.
In choosing to do wrong,
and failing to do good,
I have sinned against you
whom I should love above all things.
I firmly intend,
with your help,
to do penance,
to sin no more,
and to avoid whatever leads me to sin.
Our Savior Jesus Christ
suffered and died for us.
In his name, my God, have mercy.

Prayer to the Guardian Angel

Angel sent by God to guide me,
be my light and walk beside me;
be my guardian and protect me;
on the path of life direct me.

Morning Prayer

Almighty God,
you have given us this day:
strengthen us with your power
and keep us from falling into sin,
so that whatever we say or think or do
may be in your service and for the
    sake of your kingdom.
We ask this through Christ our Lord.
Amen.

Act of Faith

O God, we firmly believe that you are
one God in three divine Persons,
Father, Son, and Holy Spirit; we
believe that your divine Son became
man and died for our sins, and that he
will come to judge the living and the
dead. We believe these and all the
truths that the holy Catholic Church
teaches, because you have revealed
them, and you can neither deceive or
be deceived.

Act of Hope

O God, relying on your almighty
power and your endless mercy and
promises, we hope to gain pardon for
our sins, the help of your grace, and
life everlasting, through the saving
actions of Jesus Christ, our Lord and
Redeemer.

Act of Love

O God, we love you above all things,
with our whole heart and soul, because
you are all-good and worthy of all
love. We love our neighbor as
ourselves for the love of you. We
forgive all who have injured us and
ask pardon of all whom we have
injured.

The Jesus Prayer

Lord Jesus Christ,
Son of God,
have mercy on me, a sinner.
Amen.

Prayer to the Holy Spirit

Come, Holy Spirit, fill the hearts of your faithful,
And kindle in them the fire of your love.
Send forth your Spirit and they shall be created.
And you will renew the face of the earth.
Lord, by the light of the Holy Spirit
you have taught the hearts of your faithful.
In the same Spirit
help us relish what is right
and always rejoice in your consolation.
We ask this through Christ our Lord.
Amen.

I Confess

I confess to almighty God,
and to you, my brothers and sisters,
that I have sinned through my own fault
in my thoughts and in my words,
in what I have done,
and in what I have failed to do;
and I asked blessed Mary, ever virgin,
all the angels and saints,
and you, my brothers and sisters,
to pray for me to the Lord our God.

Serenity Prayer

God, grant me the serenity
to accept the things I cannot change,
the courage to change the things I can,
and the wisdom to know the difference.
Amen.

Rules Catholics Live By

The Great Commandments

"Love the Lord your God
with all your heart
with all your soul
with all your strength, and
with all your mind;
love your neighbor as you love yourself."
(Luke 10:27; Deuteronomy 6:5; Leviticus 19:18)

"You shall love the Lord your God with all your heart,
with all your soul,
with all your strength,
and with all your mind,
and your neighbor as yourself."
(Mark 12:28–31)

The Ten Commandments

1. I am the Lord, your God. You shall not have strange gods before me.
2. You shall not take the name of the Lord your God in vain.
3. Remember to keep holy the Lord's day.
4. Honor your father and your mother.
5. You shall not kill.
6. You shall not commit adultery.
7. You shall not steal.
8. You shall not bear false witness against your neighbor.
9. You shall not covet your neighbor's wife.
10. You shall not covet your neighbor's goods.

(Deuteronomy 5:6–21)

Rules Catholics Live By

Precepts of the Church

1. You shall attend Mass on Sundays and on holy days of obligation and rest from servile labor.
2. You shall confess your sins at least once a year.
3. You shall receive the Sacrament of the Eucharist at least during the Easter Season.
4. You shall observe the days of fasting and abstinence established by the Church.
5. You shall help provide for the needs of the Church.

The Beatitudes

Blessed are the poor in spirit,
    for theirs is the kingdom of heaven.
Blessed are they who mourn,
    for they will be comforted.
Blessed are the meek,
    for they shall inherit the land.
Blessed are they who hunger and thirst for righteousness,
    for they will be satisfied.
Blessed are the merciful,
    for they will be shown mercy.
Blessed are the clean of heart,
    for they will see God.
Blessed are the peacemakers,
    for they will be called children of God.
Blessed are they who are persecuted for the sake of righteousness,
    for theirs is the kingdom of heaven.

Gifts of the Holy Spirit

Wisdom

Understanding

Right judgment *(Counsel)*

Courage *(Fortitude)*

Knowledge

Reverence *(Piety)*

Wonder and Awe *(Fear of the Lord)*

Fruits of the Spirit

Charity	Generosity
Joy	Gentleness
Peace	Faithfulness
Patience	Modesty
Kindness	Self-control
Goodness	Chastity

Theological Virtues

Faith

Hope

Love

Cardinal Virtues

Prudence

Justice

Fortitude

Temperance

Works of Mercy

Corporal (for the body)

Feed the hungry.

Give drink to the thirsty.

Clothe the naked.

Shelter the homeless.

Visit the sick.

Visit the imprisoned.

Bury the dead.

Spiritual (for the spirit)

Warn the sinner.

Teach the ignorant.

Counsel the doubtful.

Comfort the sorrowful.

Bear wrongs patiently.

Forgive injuries.

Pray for the living and the dead.

What Catholics Believe

The Nicene Creed

We believe in one God,
the Father, the Almighty,
maker of heaven and earth,
of all that is seen and unseen.
We believe in one Lord, Jesus Christ,
the only Son of God,
eternally begotten of the Father,
God from God, Light from Light,
true God from true God,
begotten, not made, one in Being with the Father.
Through him all things were made.
For us men and for our salvation
he came down from heaven:
by the power of the Holy Spirit
he was born of the Virgin Mary, and became man.
For our sake he was crucified under Pontius
    Pilate;
he suffered, died, and was buried.
On the third day he rose again
in fulfillment of the Scriptures;
he ascended into heaven
and is seated at the right hand of the Father.
He will come again in glory
to judge the living and the dead,
and his kingdom will have no end.
We believe in the Holy Spirit, the Lord, the giver
    of life,
who proceeds from the Father and the Son.
With the Father and the Son he is worshiped and
    glorified.
He has spoken through the Prophets.
We believe in one holy catholic and apostolic
    Church.
We acknowledge one baptism for the forgiveness
    of sins.
We look for the resurrection of the dead,
and the life of the world to come. Amen.

Eucharistic Prayer IV

Father, we acknowledge your greatness: all your actions show your wisdom and love. You formed man in your own likeness and set him over the whole world to serve you, his creator, and to rule over all creatures. Even when he disobeyed you and lost your friendship, you did not abandon him to the power of death, but helped all men to seek and find you. Again and again you offered a convenant to man, and through the prophets taught him to hope for salvation. Father, you so loved the world that in the fullness of time you sent your only Son to be our Savior. He was conceived through the power of the Holy Spirit, and born of the Virgin Mary, a man like us in all things but sin. To the poor he proclaimed the good news of salvation, to prisoners, freedom, and to those in sorrow, joy. In fulfillment of your will he gave himself up to death; but by rising from the dead, he destroyed death and restored life. And that we might live no longer for ourselves but for him, he sent the Holy Spirit from you, Father, as his first gift to those who believe, to complete his work on earth and bring us the fullness of grace. Father, may this Holy Spirit sanctify these offerings. Let them become the body and blood of Jesus Christ our Lord as we celebrate the great mystery which he left us as an everlasting convenant.

Catholic Devotions and Practices

Holy Days of Obligation

The holy days of obligation observed in the United States are:
- Christmas, the Nativity of the Lord (December 25)
- The Solemnity of Mary Mother of God (January 1)
- Ascension of the Lord (fortieth day after Easter)
- Assumption (August 15)
- All Saints' Day (November 1)
- Immaculate Conception (December 8)

Days of Abstinence

(Days when Catholics age fourteen and over do not eat meat)

    Ash Wednesday

    Fridays in Lent

    Good Friday

Days of Fasting

(Days when Catholics age eighteen to fifty-nine eat only one full meal)

    Ash Wednesday

    Good Friday

The Rosary

The Joyful Mysteries

1. The annunciation
2. The visitation
3. The birth of Jesus
4. The presentation in the Temple
5. Mary and Joseph find Jesus in the Temple

The Sorrowful Mysteries

1. The agony in the garden
2. The scourging of Jesus
3. The crowning with thorns
4. Jesus carries his cross
5. Jesus dies on the cross

The Glorious Mysteries

1. The resurrection
2. The ascension
3. The Holy Spirit is sent upon the apostles
4. The assumption of Mary
5. Mary is crowned queen of heaven and earth

How to Pray the Rosary

1. Hold the crucifix, and pray the Apostles' Creed.
2. Pray the Lord's Prayer when holding each single bead.
3. Pray the Hail Mary on each bead in a group of three or ten. A group of ten Hail Marys is called a *decade* of the Rosary. Think of one mystery as you pray each decade.
4. After every group of Hail Marys, pray Glory to the Father.
5. Close the Rosary by praying Hail, Holy Queen.

> Hail, holy Queen, mother of mercy,
> hail, our life, our sweetness, and our hope.
> To you we cry, the children of Eve;
> to you we send up our sighs,
> mourning and weeping in this land of exile.
> Turn, then, most gracious advocate,
> your eyes of mercy toward us;
> lead us home at last
> and show us the blessed fruit of your womb, Jesus;
> O clement, O loving, O sweet Virgin Mary.

Stations of the Cross

Traditional

1. Jesus is condemned to death.
2. Jesus takes up his cross.
3. Jesus falls the first time.
4. Jesus meets his sorrowful mother.
5. Simon of Cyrene helps Jesus.
6. Veronica wipes the face of Jesus.

7. Jesus falls a second time.
8. Jesus meets the women of Jerusalem.
9. Jesus falls a third time.
10. Jesus is stripped of his clothing.
11. Jesus is nailed to the cross.

12. Jesus dies on the cross.

13. Jesus' body is removed from the cross.
14. Jesus' body is placed in the tomb.

Scriptural

1. Jesus prays in the Garden of Olives.
2. Jesus is betrayed by Judas and arrested.
3. Jesus is condemned by the Sanhedrin.
4. Jesus is denied by Peter.
5. Jesus is condemned by Pontius Pilate.
6. Jesus is scourged and crowned with thorns.
7. Jesus is made to carry the cross.
8. Simon of Cyrene helps Jesus.
9. Jesus meets the women of Jerusalem.
10. Jesus is crucified.
11. Jesus promises the kingdom to the thief who repents.
12. Jesus speaks to his mother and his friend John.
13. Jesus dies on the cross.
14. Jesus is laid in the tomb.

Prayer for the Way of the Cross

We adore you, O Christ, and we bless you,

because by your holy cross

you have redeemed the world.

The Sacraments

Sacraments of Initiation	Sacraments of Healing	Sacraments of Service
Baptism	Reconciliation	Matrimony
Confirmation	Anointing of the Sick	Holy Orders
Eucharist		

Examination of Conscience

1. Look at your life in the light of the Beatitudes, the Ten Commandments, the Great Commandment, and the precepts of the Church.
2. Ask yourself:
   - Where have I fallen short of what God wants for me?
   - Whom have I hurt?
   - What have I done that I knew was wrong?
   - What have I not done that I should have done?
   - Are there sins I neglected to mention the last time I confessed?
   - Have I done penance and tried as hard as I could to make up for past sins?
   - Have I made the necessary changes in bad habits?
   - What areas am I still having trouble with?
   - Am I sincerely sorry for all my sins?
3. In addition to the sins you are confessing, you may wish to talk about one or more of the above questions with the priest.
4. Pray for the Holy Spirit's help in making a fresh start.

The Sacrament of Reconciliation

Communal Rite of Reconciliation

1. Greeting
2. Reading from Scripture
3. Homily
4. Examination of Conscience *with* Litany of Contrition *and* the Lord's Prayer
5. Individual Confession and Absolution
6. Closing Prayer

Individual Rite of Reconciliation

1. Welcome
2. Reading from Scripture
3. Confession of sins
4. Act of Contrition
5. Absolution
6. Closing Prayer

106

Order of the Mass

Introductory Rites
1. Entrance Song
2. Greeting
3. Rite of Blessing and Sprinkling with Holy Water *or* Penetential Rite
4. Glory to God
5. Opening Prayer

Liturgy of the Word
6. First Reading (usually from the Old Testament)
7. Responsorial Psalm
8. Second Reading (from New Testament Letters)
9. Gospel Acclamation (Alleluia)
10. Gospel
11. Homily
12. Profession of Faith (Creed)
13. General Intercessions

Liturgy of the Eucharist
14. Offertory Song (Presentation of Gifts)
15. Preparation of the Bread and Wine
16. Invitation to Prayer
17. Prayer over the Gifts
18. Preface
19. Acclamation (Holy, Holy, Holy Lord)
20. Eucharistic Prayer with Acclamation
21. Great Amen

Liturgy of the Eucharist (continued)

Communion Rite   22. Lord's Prayer

23. Sign of Peace

24. Breaking of the Bread

25. Prayers before Communion

26. Lamb of God

27. Holy Communion

28. Communion Song

29. Silent Reflection or Song of Praise

30. Prayer after Communion

Concluding Rite   31. Greeting

32. Blessing

33. Dismissal

Receiving Holy Communion

To receive Holy Communion, you must be free from mortal sin. You must be sorry for any venial sin committed since your last confession. The penetential rite at the beginning of Mass is an opportunity to express your sorrow.

To honor the Lord, we fast for one hour before receiving Holy Communion. Fasting means going without food and drink, except water and medicine.

Catholics are required to receive Holy Communion at least once a year during Easter time. But it is important to receive Holy Communion often—if possible, at every Mass.

Usually, Catholics are permitted to receive Holy Communion only once a day. There are some exceptions, such as attendance at a wedding or funeral liturgy.

Name: _____ Date: _____

Crossroads Morality Final Test

True or False (2 points each)

____ 1. The Golden Rule states that you may treat others the way they treat you.

____ 2. Morality based on faith begins with love of others.

____ 3. Jesus used the image of the reign of God to describe how we should live as a family.

____ 4. Everyone shares the exact same ideas about what's right and what's wrong.

____ 5. Church laws never change.

____ 6. Being adult means being responsible for your choices.

____ 7. Catholics are not required to follow the natural moral law.

____ 8. God judges guilt or innocence at the objective level.

____ 9. Good advisors have the experience and expertise you don't have.

____ 10. The ability to reason usually starts at about age eleven or twelve.

Word Match (2 points each)

____ 1. prudence

____ 2. Golden Rule

____ 3. idolatry

____ 4. sin

____ 5. conversion

____ 6. canonization

____ 7. liberty

____ 8. everyday

____ 9. Peter Claver

____ 10. responsibility

____ 11. pride

____ 12. big

____ 13. Elizabeth Seton

____ 14. virtue

____ 15. freedom

____ 16. Church

____ 17. snap

____ 18. conscience

____ 19. Beatitudes

____ 20. holiness

A. The habit of choosing what's right

B. First American-born citizen to be declared a saint

C. Helped Black slaves in Columbia

D. The ability to carry out the choices you make

E. Type of decision that is made spontaneously, without thinking

F. Urge us to be poor in spirit, meek, merciful, and peacemakers

G. The sin of making someone or something more important than God

H. Type of decision that shapes who you become in the future

I. Official interpreter of Jesus' moral teaching

J. An offense against yourself, other people, and God

K. The ability to judge what is right and wrong

L. What everyone is called to

M. The capacity to choose

N. The official Church process of naming a saint

O. The other side of freedom

P. Turning from sin and being reconciled with God and others

Q. One of the capital sins

R. One of the signs of a good moral decision

S. Treat others as you want them to treat you

T. Type of decision that doesn't happen very often, but affects your whole life

BROWN-ROA, a division of Harcourt Brace & Company

Fill in the Blank (2 points each)

1. The _____ norms of morality are based on the natural moral law.

2. The standards by which people judge right and wrong are called _____.

3. Jesus affectionately referred to God as _____.

4. Morality based on faith means putting on the _____ and _____ of Jesus.

5. _____ prevents people from seeing anything wrong when they are cruel or unjust to nongroup members.

6. The First Commandment is about our moral obligation to _____ and to _____ God.

7. The more we choose to do good, the freer we become by cooperating with _____.

8. To avoid snap decisions, it is important to take time to _____.

9. Jesus saw reality through the eyes of _____.

10. Calling people forward and calling people back are the functions of a _____.

Short Answers (5 points each)

1. What three conditions are necessary for a sin to be mortal?

2. What did Jesus mean when he said, "Love your neighbor as yourself?"

3. How can you develop and refine your own personal conscience?

4. When it comes to making moral decisions, what are the advantages of belonging to the Church?

Student Record Sheet

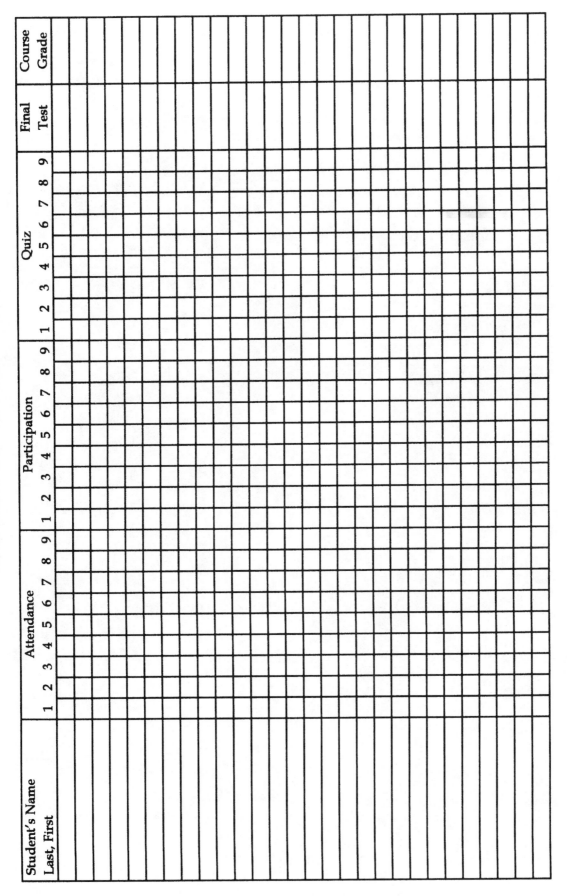

Student's Name Last, First	Attendance									Participation									Quiz									Final Test	Course Grade
	1	2	3	4	5	6	7	8	9	1	2	3	4	5	6	7	8	9	1	2	3	4	5	6	7	8	9